Thoughts about this book:

"Any objective observer knows that the two most important positions in Corrections are warden and chaplain. No other position in the field of Corrections is more misunderstood, overlooked, under-valued, and yet, so vital to the operation of a healthy correctional environment than that of chaplain. This book should be read by every student, scholar, and practitioner interested in the field of Corrections."—**Byron R. Johnson, Distinguished Professor of Social Sciences at Baylor University and author of *More God, Less Crime***

"I wish this book by Dr. Thomas Beckner had been available when I was a supervising chaplain. I would have provided it to each chaplain, and we would have had a better department. His excellent overview of *Correctional Chaplaincy* would have enabled our chaplains to understand the heritage that has brought us to this place in history.

"His focus on the four critical dimensions of chaplaincy; Personal, Pastoral, Administrative and Community provides an effective overview which leads to successful correctional chaplaincy. The concept of an Individual Institutional Ministry Plan caps off this terrific book. It is a must read for correctional chaplains, both staff chaplains and volunteer chaplains.

"In my experience chaplains who have merely a reactive ministry (just trying to react to what shows up at the office that day) have much less impact than those who have a proactive, well planned ministry. This book lays the groundwork for such a ministry which will bring great honor to our God."—**Emmett Solomon, Director of Chaplains (ret.), Texas Department of Criminal Justice**

"Having been a departmental administrator in two very different states, I can only regret that this book was not available for me and other administrators and program directors. It would be a huge mistake if this book were viewed for "chaplains only." Also, it should be an accessible resource for those responsible for leading correctional departments and institutions, volunteer and parachurch organizations, denominational agencies responsible for setting chaplaincy standards, and relevant academic departments. I don't know of anyone who is more qualified or better prepared than Dr. Tom Beckner to address chaplaincy in a thoughtful and comprehensive way."—**Dr. Ronald Powell, the first Commissioner of Corrections, New Hampshire and formerly a Deputy Commissioner in Georgia Corrections**

"Henry David Thoreau wrote: *'It takes two to speak the truth: one to speak, and another to hear.'* After twenty plus years in this profession, someone has finally written a description of chaplaincy worthy of reading. It is my hope that those who read this will listen well because Dr. Beckner speaks the truth."—**Thom McMahan, Envoy, Correctional Services Director, The Salvation Army, Wisconsin & Upper Michigan**

Dr. Beckner offers a biblically based, comprehensive look at correctional chaplaincy and identifies the critical dimensions that encompass all functions of chaplaincy. The book is both scholarly and very practical. A must read for all correctional chaplains.—**Dr. Karen Swanson, Director, Institute for Prison Ministries, Billy Graham Center, Wheaton College**

CORRECTIONAL CHAPLAINS

CORRECTIONAL CHAPLAINS

KEEPERS OF THE CLOAK

By W. Thomas Beckner

Cappella Press
Orlando, Florida

Correctional Chaplains

Keepers of the Cloak

First printing 2012

ISBN: 978-0-9851078-3-3

LCCN: 2012939975

ATTENTION CORPORATIONS, UNIVERSITIES, COLLEGES, AND PROFESSIONAL ORGANIZATIONS: Quantity discounts are available on bulk purchases of this book for educational and gift purposes, or as premiums for increasing magazine subscriptions or renewals. Special books or book excerpts can also be created to fit specific needs. For information, please contact Thomas Beckner at: **wtbeckner@att.net**

Interior and cover design by Juanita Dix
Critical Dimension graphic design by Kathy Ah Sing

Table of Contents

For Beverly

Who has been by my side throughout the circuitous path
of my ministry journey.
Always offering unwavering support and love
that has undergirded my efforts

Acknowledgments

The gestation period for this book has been rather lengthy, and I have incurred a large debt to many people who have influenced my work in correctional chaplaincy and stimulated my conceptualization of its core principles—too many to thank here. Nonetheless, I can clearly point to several to whom I owe a special expression of gratitude.

Ben Wright, the first chaplain under whom I worked. He not only modeled excellence in every dimension of chaplaincy, but also took the time to articulate the underlying principles to a young disciple hungry to learn. Thanks for birthing something within me that continues to grow many years later.

Joe Garman, a man whose ministry has served many chaplains and inmates across America, and who came alongside me early in my career. He was the first to suggest that matching my academic inclinations with the chaplaincy experiences I had could produce an educational product of value. This book is my best effort in response to that vision.

Charles Riggs, one of the most influential chaplains of his era, who somehow always had time to offer encouragement to me. As our friendship has developed through the years, we have had a number of lengthy conversations that have sharpened my thinking and enhanced my understanding of the chaplaincy profession. I hope I have done it justice. Thanks, too, for your cogent comments on an early version of this text.

Ron Powell and **Emmett Solomon**, professional colleagues from whom I have learned much about the philosophy of correctional systems and how to operate purposefully within them, and who I trusted to read this manuscript and offer honest, helpful commentary. Your insights were valuable, and they improved this work.

The numerous **students** in the college classes; the many **chaplains** I have worked with, either in a professional capacity or as attendees at training events I have facilitated; and countless **correctional administrators** who have assisted me in my endeavors. I am a sponge; I have learned from all of you, and that knowledge has worked itself into the pages of this book. In the final stages of writing, I received valuable input from several seasoned chaplains: **Stephen Hall, Joseph Pryor, Mike Reighard, Alex Taylor**, and **Al Worthley**. From the academic community, **Dr. Byron Johnson**'s timely suggestions were both generous and beneficial; and my ongoing dialogue with **Dr. Karen Swanson** helped shape several of my ideas. Thanks to each of you.

Paul Blaum, professional writer and editor, and the brother I never had. Your edit of a partial first draft, along with the conversation that followed, taught me how to tighten my writing style. Your imprint is on this final product.

Monica Beckner Robison, my daughter and gifted writer/teacher. Your perceptive reading of what I thought was a final draft of this work led to revisions of some key passages. Your students are blessed to have you guide their writing; I am blessed to have you in my life.

Beverly Beckner, my wife, who always is willing to clear the decks for some project of mine. Your faith in my abilities and your gentle nudges kept me returning to work on this book. I would never have completed it without you. Those who find it to be of some worth will have you to thank, as well as me.

Foreword

When I was introduced to Chaplain Tom Beckner in 1980, he was already leading in a robust chaplaincy service in Georgia. In each succeeding decade, Dr. Beckner increased his knowledge and skill to become the foremost voice of advocacy in support of prison ministry nationwide.

Dr. Beckner combines his academic acumen with the gift of his calling to serve the spiritual needs of inmates in America. His unique in-depth, nonjudgmental openness to prisoners has given him an unparalleled pinnacle from which to view both prison and jail chaplaincy.

This book is the result of the author's ability to bring narrative to the history, value, and essence of chaplaincy presence in these settings. His informed and accurate assessment of the present state of ministry to our nation's inmates gives validity to the opinion that this is a critically crucial moment for the future of chaplaincy to the incarcerated.

You will appreciate the detailed reporting of the limiting factors faced by present chaplaincy providers as well as the bold remedies needed to overcome these factors for effectiveness today.

Tom's dedication to the development of this monumental book will be applauded as a benchmark text for both established and new vocational chaplains entering the chaplaincy corps.

Don't hesitate to absorb the content of this work and offer it for reading to every level of institutional, denominational, and local church leaders. It will enhance your grip of the effectiveness of "keeping the cloak."

Dr. Charles R. Riggs
Director of Chaplaincy Services (Ret.)
Federal Bureau of Prisons

Introduction

One of the most engaging stories found in the gospels is that of the demon-possessed man. All three of the synoptic gospel writers tell the tale, although Mark's version—in the fifth chapter of his book (*vs. 1–20*)—is the most complete. This account is a first century forerunner of a scenario we find acted out daily in the communities of contemporary America. In fact, it could easily serve as a metaphor of our times.

The region of Decapolis (i.e., "10 cities") had a crime problem. Their problem, unlike that of most communities today, was centered in the behavior of just one man—a raving lunatic who roamed the countryside terrorizing the citizenry. Matthew's account tells us he was violent; Luke notes that he was given to running through the cities naked. Mark comments on his self-destructive tendencies: He would take stones and cut himself. He lived in the cemetery of those days, limestone caves—catacombs—which are a prominent geographical feature of that area. Daily, we are told, he could be heard crying out with a loud, terrifying voice. The citizens of the area lived in constant fear of this uncontrollable, demon-possessed man. Doesn't this scene sound a bit like some communities in America today?

> *"Many Americans live in fear of the criminal element around them. This fear is fueled by a media adept at making them uncomfortable without offering any solution beyond "tune in tomorrow at this same time for an update."*

The terrified citizens had attempted to fight back, capture this fellow, and put an end to his crazed behavior. On more than one occasion, they had managed to seize him, hold him down, and put chains on him. But this madman was so strong that he tore the chains from his body and the irons from his feet and continued his reign of terror. He was a wretched piece of humanity, apparently beyond redemption, and he held the entire region captive to their fear of his actions. This, too, sounds suspiciously contemporary, like the lead story of an evening news program.

Many Americans live in fear of the criminal element around them. This fear is fueled by a media adept at making them uncomfortable without offering any solution beyond "tune in tomorrow at this same time for an update." Pervasive fear drives Americans to demand protection from their elected officials—a protection that usually translates into newer, more secure jails and a steady stream of new prison beds. But those modern sophisticated chains offer no relief either, and so like the citizens of Decapolis, we continue to live with our fear. Our communities remain captives to the seemingly lunatic behaviors of the criminal element who live among us.

But Jesus came to Decapolis one day! From that day, neither the region nor the poor uncontrollable man living in the tombs nearby was ever the same. This same result can be true today. When Jesus, embodied in the form of a divinely called minister, arrives in a community, those communities can be transformed into safer, less fearful places. The people in those communities who allow themselves to be touched by the healing balm of Gilead receive new, redeemed lives in Christ Jesus.

> *Chaplains bear witness that iron bars and barbed-wired topped fences will not remove our fear because those devices ultimately respond only to symptoms and ignore the root causes of crime. Merely locking people away without attending to the inner psychological, social, and spiritual forces that drive their behavior is a strategy doomed to continued failure.*

Notice the progression of events as Mark relates it. The demon-possessed man saw Jesus from afar and came running to Him, throwing himself at the feet of the Master, and crying out, "What do you want with me, Jesus …?" (*vs. 6, NIV*). What a picture of contrasts! The Prince of Peace standing opposite this dirty, scarred, naked law violator. What did Jesus want? His mission was simple: to offer the man freedom from his bondage and a new life. We see similar pictures today: correctional ministers, possessors of Jesus' liberating truth, dedicating their lives to serving the undesirables who live behind the iron doors of our nation's jails and prisons.

To be sure, the terror of Decapolis was not a friendly neighbor with whom to be reasoned. Neither are the men and women who are confined in our jails and prisons placed there because they sang too loud in church! There was a real threat then, and there is today. But Jesus was willing to look beneath that dirty, half-naked body; to peer behind those wild and empty eyes; to approach this shell of a being not as a problem-solving object, but as a person—as someone of worth. Jesus recognized that the man's behavior was symptomatic of a much deeper problem, and He spoke to the source of that problem—the demons that ruled the man.

Chaplains bear witness that iron bars and barbed-wired topped fences will not remove our fear because those devices ultimately respond only to symptoms and ignore the root causes of crime. Merely locking people away without attending to the inner psychological, social, and spiritual forces that drive their behavior is a strategy doomed to continued failure. When men and women take seriously Christ's mandate to visit those in prison (*Matt. 25:31–46*), they not only visit Him there, but in a very real sense, they become the Christ to the person they encounter. Prison chaplains and their ministry associates confront the demonic, and like Jesus, they quickly discern that the enemies they face are not evil people, but the evil influences that rule those people's lives. Notice what happens in Mark's story. Jesus addresses the underlying source of the problem, and right behavior follows. When the citizens of Decapolis hear what's happened, they rush to the scene only to find the former demon-possessed man sitting calmly, "dressed and in his right mind" (*vs. 15*). He had been restored to human society. Getting to the root of the problem—spiritual enslavement—has the potential to produce behavioral change!

But interestingly enough, the citizens of the community aren't pleased. In the process of healing the man, Jesus had upset the routine to which everyone was accustomed. So much so that they begged Him to leave the region! They had been living in fear for years, and Jesus had just cleansed their community from the very object of their fears. One would think they would be ecstatic; instead, the Scriptures tell us, they were afraid (*vs. 15*). Afraid? Hadn't they already been living in constant fear? Indeed they had, but this new fear was of a different kind. This was the fear that strikes deep into the hearts of people whose entire worldview has just been turned upside down. For as strange as it may seem, they had learned to live with their fear; they had adjusted to it and had become comfortable in spite of that fear.

Mark's rendition of this encounter is, in many ways, a metaphor of American communities in the twenty-first century. Despite our complaints about crime, we Americans have grown accustomed to it and desensitized by it. We glue our eyes to the media reports of some current celebrity's encounter with the criminal justice system, hanging on every word so we'll have something to talk about when we get together with our friends. We watch news accounts of robberies, drug busts, or domestic shootings and sigh deeply, shaking our heads in resignation as we tune the television to our favorite violence-riddled crime show, never once imagining a world where violence and crime are not the norm. Too often, it's only when crime strikes close to us—when it threatens *our* property, *our* safety, or the lives of *our* friends or loved ones—that we see it in realistic terms.

The inhabitants of Decapolis, too, had grown accustomed to hearing the screams of the demoniac, to catching an occasional glimpse of him as he ran through the streets, yet they were smugly comfortable with their own law-abiding behavior. When they witnessed the power of Jesus unleashed on this man, they were afraid of what might happen if that power were directed at them. For their lives, too, were subject to reversal. Thus, they were quite content and said, "Thank you very much, Jesus, but no thanks. Now please leave us alone!"

Many people in our communities fear any successes produced by ministry to offenders. When our neighbors witness the changed lives of ex-offenders, they have to rethink their cynicisms and acknowledge the shortcomings of their belief systems. Most importantly, they must come to grips with the fact that Jesus is truly capable of transforming lives, and therefore they can no longer accept their own failure to live up to His will for their lives. If Jesus possesses real power, then everyone must move away from his or her comfort zone.

The truth is that few people in our communities seem eager to hear about successful ministries among offenders. Such success strikes at the very heart of their distorted thinking about crime and criminals, and they won't easily abandon those thought patterns. They are quick to support retribution but slow to embrace forgiveness.

Something else irritated the good citizens of Decapolis about Jesus' actions that day. He got into the pocketbooks of that community! When Jesus cast the demons out of the lunatic, they entered a herd of nearby pigs, which then rushed headlong into the sea and were drowned (*vs. 12–13*). Two thousand pigs died that day, all being raised by the swine herders for profit. These herders did a little math and quickly concluded that if Jesus stayed around very long, they were out of business. So they asked Him to leave. Jesus cared for men; they cared for property—and the price of one man's redemption was too high. They decided they would rather live with their fear than lose the pig market.

Unfortunately, the same instinct is operative today. Crime is a multibillion-dollar business with countless private vendors deriving huge revenue from it, and large state and federal bureaucracies structured around responses to it. Indeed, the corrections industry is one of the largest in this country. Much of the business community does not really want to see crime eradicated; they only want it to be effectively controlled and managed. Simply put, they want to keep their pigs. Every time a prison is built, it is sold to the host community as a reliable provider of solid, long-term jobs. Examples abound of rural, economically depressed areas that have aggressively lobbied their state correctional agencies in an effort to secure a prison site in their county. It's unfortunate that so many people are employed by an industry that thrives on the brokenness of its neighbors.

While the recent economic recession and a leveling off of the growth in crime statistics has slowed the building binge, a strong commitment to incarceration as a solution to many social problems continues to dominate national agendas. As Eric Schlosser pointed out in his provocative 1998 article, "The prison-industrial complex is not only a set of interest groups and institutions. It is also a state of mind. The lure of big money is corrupting the nation's criminal-justice system, replacing notions of public service with a drive for higher profits" (Schlosser 54–55). Effective ministry to inmates could place jobs in jeopardy and profits at risk, and many people prefer jobs and profits to reclaimed lives of individuals they don't know or care about.

Yet even after Jesus got into the boat and sailed away, that changed demoniac—he who used to live in the graveyard and hurl screams that echoed across the hills—was influencing his neighbors. According to verse 20, he "began to tell in the Decapolis how much Jesus had done for him. All the people were amazed." We can well imagine the scenario. The wary citizens are fascinated by the sight of the scarred but clothed and sane newcomer to their town. They keep their distance from him, curious but unwilling to come too close for fear that he might suddenly revert to his former behavior, or at the very least, somehow contaminate them. Finally, one particularly brave or overly curious man asks the inevitable question.

> *Jesus continues to touch men and women who have been slaves to Satan-led lives of crimes, transforming them into productive citizens, good neighbors, and witnesses to the power of God.*

"You're the fellow that used to live up in the tombs, aren't you? The one who used to…." his voice trails off.

"Yes," the man replies. "That was me."

"Well, what in the world happened to you?"

The once wretched creature replies, "I'd love to tell you about it. One day I met a man called Jesus." Here the new follower of Christ offers his testimony to another.

Those engaged for any length of time in a ministry to offenders and their families can share similar scenarios, for Jesus continues to touch men and women who have been slaves to Satan-led lives of crimes, transforming them into productive citizens, good neighbors, and witnesses to the power of God. Miracles are still performed by those who believe in them and who come in the name of Jesus. Correctional chaplains are called by God to be such people. Strategically placed within the strongholds of evil, they daily minister to men and women not unlike the Terror of Decapolis, and in so doing minister to the surrounding free-world communities as well.

This book will familiarize the reader with the work of chaplaincy in contemporary correctional settings. I will assume that, since the reader has selected a text in this specialized ministry area, he or she already understands the scriptural and theological basis for a ministry to offenders; thus, this book will not offer an extensive treatment of those matters. Instead, I will begin our study by briefly reviewing the history of Christian correctional chaplaincy (Chapter One) and how it has developed within the American criminal justice system (Chapter Two). Then I will move to a broad overview of the work of chaplaincy, reviewing some of the scant literature of the profession and examining the critical premises on which it must rest (Chapter Three).

Next, I will present a structural model that incorporates the various dimensions of chaplaincy and can serve as a template for any institutional ministry (Chapter Four). Following that, I will more closely examine each of the four critical dimensions of chaplaincy: 1) personal, 2) pastoral, 3) administrative, and 4) community (Chapters Five through Eight). Having explored these components of chaplaincy, I will then suggest a process for creating an individualized ministry plan that conforms to the specific demographics of an institution and its inmate population (Chapter Nine). Our study will close with a call for a revitalized approach to this crucial ministry arena and suggest some specific strategies for its future (Chapter Ten).

This book focuses on the formal position of the institutional chaplain and the individual officially designated for that role. I will attempt to incorporate all the potential components of chaplaincy—not just those that have traditionally been fulfilled—and I will examine the relationship of chaplaincy to the Church in the community. Correctional chaplaincy has already experienced several transitions during its history, as we shall see. This book isn't intended to create yet another best-version definition that meets certain needs in the current environment. Instead, it is an attempt to offer a functional model that incorporates the wide range of job roles within an enduring paradigm and to suggest a template for ministry within any correctional setting that allows for institutional-specific strategies, while at the same time fulfilling permanent critical values of the position.

*My thoughts for this introductory essay based on Mark's gospel account were inspired by a sermon entitled, "The Terror of Gadera," written by Joe Garman, President of American Rehabilitation Ministries (http://www.arm.org).

REFERENCES

Schlosser, Eric. (1998). The Prison-Industrial Complex. *Atlantic Monthly*. December, 51–77.

Chapter One

The Historical Roots of Correctional Chaplaincy

To be identified as a chaplain is to be a part of a rich tradition that finds its roots in the fourth century. The word itself is derived from the Latin *cappellanus*, a title given to the priest who served as a custodian of sacred relics, which in turn was derived from *capella*, a "short cloak."mThe use of the term appears to have been first applied to the clergy in charge of the cloak of St. Martin of Tours (c. 316-397).

> *The tradition of St. Martin is a particularly fitting backdrop for the men and women who bring comfort, hope, and a message of redemption to the outcasts in America's jails and prisons. Like St. Martin, chaplains take seriously the words of Jesus recorded in Matt. 25: 36-37:*

One day, legend has it, St. Martin met a ragged beggar on the road and, out of compassion, tore his own cloak in half and gave it to the beggar. Later, Martin had a vision in which Christ appeared to him wrapped in the beggar's half of his cloak. Martin's half was later preserved, initially carried into battles by Frankish kings and later kept in a building that became known as a chapel. Eventually, anyone assigned to watch over the sanctuary where this cape or any other relic was housed came to be called a *chaplain*—the keeper of the cloak. By extension, in modern times, the term has been assigned to those clergy who minister in specialized institutions such as hospitals, the military, and prisons. More recently, it has been used to designate clergypersons who serve any discrete groups of people in communities outside the framework of the local church or parish.

The tradition of St. Martin is a particularly fitting backdrop for the men and women who bring comfort, hope, and a message of redemption to the outcasts in America's jails and prisons. Like St. Martin, chaplains take seriously the words of Jesus recorded in Matt. 25: 36-37: "For I was hungry and you gave me something to eat, I was thirsty and you gave me something to drink, I was a stranger and you invited me in, I needed clothes and you clothed me, I was sick and you looked after me, I was in prison, and you came to visit me."

Though we have some early historical references to the imprisonment of individuals, these reflect treatment of the exceptional rather than the ordinary criminal. Most early societies couldn't afford to support extensive prisons, so they utilized them only for the special case. For example, Scripture records that the prison to which Joseph was sent was "the place where the king's prisoners were confined" *(Gen. 39:20)*. Often, punishments were harsh; offenders were either physically maimed or executed. But sometimes, as in the case of political enemies (the king's prisoners) authorities couldn't just cut off a hand or brand the forehead of their adversary and let him return to society—the foe would continue to be a threat. Moreover, it was seldom wise to execute a popular person; such an action would only create a martyr and stir up the victim's followers. So, political prisoners had to be held in some location indefinitely (Keve 33-34).

For most of history, incarceration has been used only as a means of detention, holding prisoners awaiting trial or the enactment of their sentences. For instance, Roman law forbade its use as punishment. Imprisonment—as the primary means of enforcing customs, laws, and mores of a people—is a relatively modern device. The use of prison sentences as a standard means of punishment appeared somewhat later in history when the worth of the individual had become more highly regarded. It was the introduction of Christianity, with its call for drastic change in social conditions and attitudes, which really ushered in the concept of prisons.

From the reign of Constantine (A.D. 306-37), clergy, monks, and other clerics fell under the jurisdiction of church courts. These men were usually the most well educated and therefore considered of special value to society, so the prevailing notion was that if they had to be punished, they should not be "wasted." Thus, in the 12th century, a practice known as *Benefit of Clergy* was built into the legal system so that those officials tried by church court received less severe penalties than their fellow citizens. Later, when non-ecclesiastics began to be educated, the benefit was extended to all who could read. This practice was finally abolished in England in 1827 (35).

The prophet Hosea viewed God's wrath as an instrument of punishment that both purified and redeemed an unfaithful Israel. Emphasizing this theme of purification through suffering, the church courts came to subject wrongdoers to reclusion—solitary cellular confinement—not just in order to punish the offender, but to provide conditions under which penitence was most likely to occur. This, then, was an early forerunner of the penitentiary. In some instances, monks were transferred to remote "satellite houses," monasteries and abbeys which some historians believe began to be identified primarily as punitive facilities. During the Inquisition era, some accused heretics, spared from execution, were imprisoned for life.

It was during the Middle Ages that imprisonment for criminal activity became normative. Instrumental in the development of this phenomenon was the disintegration of feudalism. The Black Death of 1348 decimated half of the work force of Central Europe, creating a tremendous upheaval among serfs and precipitating a migration to cities. There, vagrant laws were commonly passed in a futile effort to prevent working class men from roaming about in search of higher wages (37). However, cities continued to grow amid the influx of serfs who migrated to urban areas to find work. Often, though, employment was not secured, and the result was a rapid increase in vagrancy. A natural by-product of this process was increased criminal activity, and the emergence of local jails—squalid places where men, women, and children were confined together with no regard for the nature of their offenses or for their individual safety.

Churchmen in the British Isles, attempting to create humanitarian alternatives to harsh corporal punishments and executions, were leaders in developing the *workhouse* as a means of providing temporary housing for vagrants, debtors, and other petty offenders. The first of these, opened in Scotland in 1557, was a converted palace which became known as Bridwell because of its location near St. Bridget's Well. Designed to take vagrants and the destitute off the street while at same time introducing them to a work ethic—the central feature of the *workhouse*—this model was copied by cities throughout Europe. Each of the institutions soon filled with beggars and petty criminals, but gradually the workhouses came to be used exclusively for more serious offenders. Before long, they deteriorated through overuse, lack of public support, and poor operational standards (38).

Colonial America made extensive use of physical punishment, a practice inherited from its European ancestors. In the small villages that made up most of the New World, a rigid sense of sin and a strict criminal code were equally prevalent. The colonial system emphasized cohesiveness, and severe measures were imposed upon those who violated community rules. In the Massachusetts Bay Colony, for instance, a 1641 code provided the death penalty for 12 offenses, with two more capital offenses added a few years later (44). Although these severe measures were seldom utilized, corporal punishment was common. Stocks and pillories were designed to inflict both pain and public humiliation. Once again, it was a Christian influence which reacted against this type of punishment.

In 1682, William Penn, Quaker governor of Pennsylvania, drew up a code of laws that inaugurated the concept of confinement as punishment. Known as the *Great Code*, this document differed so radically from the practices of the mother country, England, that Queen Anne soon disallowed it. But later Enlightenment reformers picked up threads of Penn's thoughts and integrated them into their penal reform movements.

Most prominent of these was John Howard, a wealthy Englishman. Having been appointed High Sheriff of Bedfordshire, he found the conditions of his local Bedford Gaol ("jail") shockingly inhumane. Consequently, he set out on a tour of Europe to study prison conditions on the continent.

Thus began a lifetime commitment to improve conditions in the English penal system. In the best of the prisons he visited, Howard saw models that attempted corrective discipline rather than mere confinement, and he began to envision institutions which reformed the individuals they housed. He also saw a connection between that process and Quakerism.

> Howard believed a convict's process of reformation was similar to the spiritual awakening of a believer at a Quaker meeting. In the vigil of silence, both the convict and believer hear the inner voice of conscience and feel the transforming power of God's love. (Cowart 32)

Similarly, Howard influenced Pennsylvania Quakers. There, a newly revised state constitution (1776) already contained a statement of intention to enact penal reform when Howard's now-famous book, *The State of Prisons*, was published the next year.

The timing of this event was propitious. First of all, their recent victory over England made Americans eager to divest themselves of English traditions and establish their own method of responding to social problems. Secondly, the same Enlightenment spirit that inspired framers of the *Declaration of Independence* influenced the leaders of the new nation to believe in the perfectibility of its people and institutions. The notion of reforming criminals was an integral part of the growing spirit of the country. Thirdly, Quakers were repulsed by notions of harsh punishments, so severe criminal codes were distasteful to them. Finally, Christians were quick to embrace Howard's insistence on humane conditions within the prisons. Thus, Pennsylvania became the initiator of reform that was to change the course of American (and perhaps world) penal history.

Then in 1786, Pennsylvania rewrote its state code to reflect William Penn's earlier *Great Code*, emphasizing punishment by labor in the penitentiary rather than corporal or capital punishment (Keve 68). One year later, a group of Quakers and friends associated themselves as the Philadelphia Society for Alleviating the Miseries of Public Prisons, an organization which continues to the present day under the name of The Pennsylvania Prison Society. The Society later published an influential tract which promoted John Howard's ideas, suggested that Pennsylvania make its prisons "places of correction" and specifically proposed reformation of the Walnut

Street Jail in Philadelphia (Cowart 33). The Society also advocated for the prisoner's right to have access to community religious leaders. That same year, 1790, the Pennsylvania legislature made this jail the world's first penitentiary (Cowart 33).

> *Christian jail and prison ministers frequently point with great pride to the fact that prisons were initiated by Quakers and that the notion of penitence was central to their corrective strategy. But those same ministers must acknowledge that the prison system failed to reform any significant percentage of individuals.*

Although the Walnut Street Jail was imitated in several other states, commitment to incarceration as a means of punishment increased in the years that followed, and it soon became apparent that new and larger institutions were necessary. With the construction of the Auburn Prison in New York (1817) and Eastern State Penitentiary in Philadelphia (1829), rival penitentiary systems were born. But while specific architectural features and the efficacy of strict isolation were debated, both assumed that the convict could overcome his faults through industrious habits and could find in Scriptures the principles of right and wrong that could change his ways. More importantly, the concept of deprivation of liberty as appropriate punishment was never questioned, and the evolving prison system accepted it as axiomatic. Specifically, the early reformers embraced four assumptions that dominated penal philosophy for the next century.

- The causes of crime are located within the individual.
- People should be punished for their inappropriate actions.
- Behavior is modifiable.
- Isolated institutions are the appropriate setting in which to modify those behaviors.

Chaplains—community-based pastors who served without pay—performed a vital service in this environment.

Christian jail and prison ministers frequently point with great pride to the fact that prisons were initiated by Quakers and that the notion of penitence was central to their corrective strategy. But those same ministers must acknowledge that the prison system failed to reform any significant percentage of individuals. Attempts to explain this phenomenon are seldom satisfactory. J.T.L. James, in his excellent history of the Canadian prison chaplaincy, *A Living Tradition: Penitentiary Chaplain*, addresses this issue with great discernment. James points out that penance is a fundamental Christian concept, a practice found in the earliest records of the church. Tertullian (160-220 AD) records such penitential acts as fasting, dressing in sack cloth and rags, and harsh treatment of the body. St. Thomas Aquinas (1225-1274) describes penance as ". . . the payment of the temporal punishment due on account of the offense committed against God by sins" (James 32). The practice of segregating a select group of the religious community for the purposes of doing penance, as well as the principle of confinement in a cell as a way to encourage making amends is recorded in other early Christian writings.

The central question, as James phrases it, is: "Can convicted criminals be treated as if they were penitents seeking reconciliation with God against whom they had sinned? Are they really seeking restoration to fellowship in the community of the faithful which they had forfeited by their sin?" (33). James answers the question by first pointing out that monks, unlike convicts, entered monastic life voluntarily and willingly submitted to the church's penitential sanctions. Other Christians who committed public sin and were disciplined by the church valued membership in the religious community and accepted that discipline as the price for reentry to that community. Criminals, on the other hand, do not enter prison voluntarily, nor do they usually share the values of those who impose secular penance upon them. Furthermore, they are not bonded to the civil community in the same way as the Christian is to the Church (33).

Prison reformers apparently assumed that what worked for sinners would work for criminals. But as Gerald Austin McHugh points out, they misunderstood the concept of penance and misapplied its principles.

> . . . the Church's approach to punishment and repentance, at least in theory (The Inquisition and the worst monastic prisons were the major exceptions.), was based on the belief that penances (punishments) were effective only when the sin-

ner had voluntarily repented. The power of human freedom made it impossible to compel someone to feel truly repentant for sin. Repentance must be a free act of the will; otherwise, it would not be the result of sorrow or remorse, but of fear or self-interest. Punishment was something which followed repentance, as a penance, a sign of purification and resolve not to sin again. The spiritual value of a penance not performed voluntarily was slight. The penitentiary model reversed this order. Punishment was to precede and lead the sinner to repentance. The sinner must be made to repent. What the penitential reformers failed to recognize, however, was the power of the human will, and the absurdity of trying to force offenders into true repentance by denying them liberty. Ironically, while the penitentiary denied prisoners' physical freedom, and had deleterious psychological effects, it failed to eradicate their most important freedom—freedom to resist spiritual coercion. (McHugh 43)

The Christian reformers of the late 18th and early 19th century also either ignored or were unaware that by most assessments, the monastic penitentiaries were also failures. What failed to work for monks was unlikely to succeed with criminals; still, the theory that reformation was best achieved through confinement was hard to dislodge, regardless of the degree of ineffectiveness. Nonetheless, Christian chaplains faithfully continued their ministries inside these penitentiaries in an effort to help facilitate change in the lives of offenders.

Eventually, the tremendous growth of prison populations in nearly every state led to overcrowding. At the same time, funding these institutions was seldom a public priority. The result was that prisons were forced to operate without even basic amenities such as heating and lighting; food was often very sparse; and physical comforts frequently lacking. Once again, reform groups introduced new concepts intended to improve prison conditions and at the same time restore the potential of such places to initiate constructive change in the lives of their inhabitants. Those efforts, too, were rooted in Christian principles and, once again, it was chaplains, volunteering their services, who advocated for improved conditions while at the same time attempting to bring prisoners to repentance.

Initially, the problems were addressed through separate facilities for youthful offenders. These *reform schools*, once developed, provide the impetus for *reformatories* intended for housing of young adult offenders 16 to 30 years of age. The first of these was opened in 1877 in Elmira, New York and served as a model for similar institutions constructed in many states during the years that followed. Zebulon Brockway was appointed the first superintendent of the Elmira facility, a man who had established a reputation at the Detroit House of Correction by progressive measures such as grading systems for types of inmates, educational programming, and an incentive wage system (Keve 89). At Elmira, he again divided his inmates into grades—levels of privileges—and introduced a system of *marks* that could be earned. These permitted the prisoner to increase his privilege level and eventually earn a release. Strong educational programs and trade training were also facets of the Elmira program. Significantly, a few years earlier, while superintendent at a Rochester penitentiary, Brockway had experienced a religious conversion that profoundly influenced his subsequent career. He never lost belief that prisoners could be reclaimed (91).

It was Brockway who in October, 1870 delivered what is considered the most influential address to delegates of the first National Prison Congress (later the American Correctional Association) convening in Cincinnati. Titled "The Ideal of a True Prison System for a State," the speech is saturated with references to Brockway's faith and ends with a stirring plea for creating institutions based on Christian ideals.

> The ideal of a true prison system, in the great scope of its influence, in the spirit and principles upon which it is based, in its grand two-fold aim, in its plan of organization and legislation, and in the details of its administration, is the *christian ideal*, in all the breadth and blessedness of that term. Let us then, lend our influence and our aid to plant such a system, not only in one state, but in every state, and throughout the world, being assured that when we have found the "philosophy of the plan of salvation" for the feeble and fallen of our fellow-creatures, we shall have found God's plan for saving the race, and may

feel the force of those Divine words, "Inasmuch as ye have done it unto one of the least of these my brethren, ye have done it unto me." (Wines 65)

Inspired by such idealistic visions, the Congress adopted 41 principles around which to organize future reformation endeavors. These principles declared that society was responsible for reforming prisoners; that reformation was best accomplished through indeterminate sentences where prisoners earned release by demonstrating changed behavior; that religion, as well as education and vocational training was necessary to achieve rehabilitation of offenders; and that post-release assistance by the states was crucial to the success of discharged prisoners. As one prison historian comments, "Overwhelmed with inspired addresses, with prayer and song and much exhortation, even the hardheaded wardens were carried up for a mountaintop experience" (McKelvey 91). These ideals, though only partially implemented and seldom achieved, nonetheless dominated the thinking of prison officials for the next century, forming the basis for the rehabilitation ideal that became the operative model for most correctional systems until the mid 1970's.

> *Central to rehabilitative programming concepts was the medical model. The criminal was no longer viewed as a sinner, but as one who was ill and who needed treatment rather than religious instruction; the prison became a moral hospital, equipped with programmatic capacities based on positivist principles.*

The Prison Congress of 1870 initiated a wave of correctional programming supervised by an increasing number of specialists: psychologists, counselors, educators, and the like. This signaled the beginning of the professionalization of such institutional positions that in time became imbedded staffing patterns. Though many of Brockway's reform strategies were never fully implemented, the rehabilitative ideal thrived, especially in the years immediately following World War II. Fresh from a victorious campaign to rid the world of dehumanizing dictatorships, American social reformers turned their attention to internal problems, one of which was the reformation of offenders. Central to rehabilitative programming concepts was the medical model. The criminal was no longer viewed as a sinner, but as one who was ill and who needed treatment rather than religious instruction; the prison became a moral hospital, equipped with programmatic capacities based on positivist principles. It was in this era that chaplaincy positions became normative in correctional settings, and Andrew Skotnicki argues that they were highly influential in the emerging correctional philosophies.

> . . . chaplains and religious leaders of the mid-nineteenth century inaugurated the positivist shift in penal thinking that created the conditions for the Social Gospel phenomenon in Protestant Christianity. This development transferred the evangelical emphasis on personal conversion to a need to create new institutions responsible for generating the reign of God on earth. (Skotnicki 7)

Gradually, though, amid the growing professionalism of correctional leadership that rapidly began to configure around distinct institutional positions, the religious rhetoric that had so influenced the Congress's guiding principles became diminished through the tenants of social science, and both the role and influence of chaplains became more restricted. Sanford Bates, first director of the Bureau of Prisons and later president of the American Correctional Association expressed the significance of this change:

> The prison school had been taken over by trained educationalists. Family contacts were handled by the social workers and the libraries staffed by trained librarians. Apparently there was nothing else but religion for the chaplain to busy himself about, and that could be done on Sunday in an hour or two. (Bates, 163)

Moreover, state treasuries were not bottomless wells from which correctional agencies could draw unlimited funds, especially when the recipients were people convicted of crimes against the taxpayers who supplied those resources. Ultimately, questions about the validity of reformation philosophy and the notion of rehabilitation led to assessments of program efficacies. The most ambitious of these assessments was conducted by a team of researchers led by Robert Martinson. The group analyzed 231 studies published between 1945 and 1967 of a broad variety of treatment programs—religious, recreational, psychological, educational, etc.—and evaluated them on the basis of such principles as recidivism, drug and alcohol relapse, and community readjustments. Prior to the appearance of the complete report, Martinson published an article summarizing the study that asserted, "With few and isolated exceptions, the rehabilitative efforts that have been reported so far have had no appreciable effect on recidivism" (Martinson 25).

Though Martinson's report was attacked by other critics (with some justification) as being distortive and grossly misrepresentative, his essay created a sensation at a time when politicians and media were responding to public fears about crime. As Harvard University professor James Q. Wilson noted:

> Martinson did not discover that rehabilitation was of little value in dealing with crime so much as he administered a highly visible *coup de grace*. By bringing out into the open the long-standing scholarly skepticism about most rehabilitation programs, he prepared the way for a revival of an interest in the deterrent, incapacitative, and retributive purposes of the criminal justice system. (Wilson 4)

The revival of interest in these punishment philosophies signaled the beginning of the end for many treatment programs consistent with Scripture that had served as the point of involvement with the system for large numbers of Christian volunteers. The retributive justice model that emerged viewed both rehabilitation and deterrence merely as by-products of a system whose fundamental mission was to ensure *just desserts*.

It is clear also that the death of the rehabilitative ideal within the correctional community was paralleled by a gradual but persistent erosion of commitment to institutional chaplaincy programs that have now come to be identified as only one of several components in a matrix of treatment alternatives, each of which is expected to have some measurable outcomes.

This shift also introduced more questions about the nature of the chaplain and his or her institutional role—the subject of discussion for the balance of this book.

REFERENCES

Bates, Sanford. (1938). *Prisons and Beyond*. New York: MacMillan.

Cowart, John L. (1996). *The Prison Minister's Handbook*. San Jose, CA: Resource Publications, Inc.

James, J.T.L. (1990). *A Living Tradition: Penitentiary Chaplain*. Ottawa: Chaplaincy Division, Correctional Service of Canada.

Keve, Paul W. (1981). *Corrections*. New York: John Wiley & Sons.
Martinson, Robert. (1974). *What Works? Questions and Answers About Prison Reform*. The Public Interest. 35: 22–54.

McHugh, Gerald Austin. (1978). *Christian Faith and Criminal Justice*. New York: Paulist Press.

McKelvey, Blake. (1977). *American Prisons: A History of Good Intentions*. Montclair, NJ: Patterson Smith Publishing.

Skotnicki, Andrew. (2000). *Religion and the Development of the American Penal System*. Lanham, MD: University Press of America.

Wilson, James Q. (1980). *'What Works?' Revisited: New Findings on Criminal Rehabilitation*. Public   Interest. 61: 3–17.

Wines, E.C., ed. (1871). *Transactions of the National Congress on Penitentiary and Reform Discipline*. Albany: Weed, Parsons and Co. 1970. Rpt. American Correctional Assoc.

Chapter Two

The Changing Face of
Correctional Chaplaincy*

As belief in secular solutions to criminal behavior gained promi-
nence, the role of religion in the reformation of offenders
gradually diminished. In spite of its lengthy history of providing
religious leadership on a voluntary basis, the Church had little influence on
prison staff design. Consequently, the system was slow to establish professionally identified chaplains as part of the programmatic team. Even when
chaplains eventually began to emerge in staffing patterns, they had ancillary
duties ranging from teaching and maintaining libraries to serving as recre-
ation coordinators (see Skotnicki). Voluntary pastoral attention remained
the norm well into the twentieth century, even as other new prison categories of paid staff emerged.

During the middle part of the twentieth century, ministers serving in
correctional settings saw the advantage of a professional organization that
would serve their cause. The American Correctional Chaplains Association
(ACCA) was formed in 1885 as the first affiliate of what has become the
American Correctional Association (Friedman). From it, later descendants
were birthed—the American Protestant Correctional Chaplains Association (APCCA), the American Catholic Correctional Chaplains Association

15

(ACCCA), and the American Jewish Correctional Chaplains Association (AJCCA). Gradually, too, as the social sensitivities of the mainline churches in America increased, more ministerial specialties began to form. No longer was the "pastor-with-pulpit" the sole identification of a legitimate ministerial calling. Specialized settings such as prisons, the military, mental health institutions, and hospitals became a worthy focus for the organized religious bodies of America. With the increasing acceptance of those clergy focusing on something other than the traditional church pastorate came new developmental educational tracks to prepare these uniquely positioned ministers. This specialized education, designed to prepare the minister serving in institutional settings developed with the full blessing of established, mainline American churches.

One such focused educational preparation, Clinical Pastoral Education (CPE), became the dominant model as addendum training to the seminary curriculum for those choosing ministry in a nontraditional clergy or pastoral role. Primarily, this vehicle applied to Protestant denominations, many of which developed a set of qualifications for their clergy to be certified for ministry in specialized settings. CPE became a non-equivocal, mandated standard established by these Protestant groups. Soon, however, CPE took on a life of its own and became less and less subject to church standards that included expectations for a co-existing theological core curriculum.

The Protestant denominations that embraced and promoted the CPE educational model influenced institutional treatment programs to establish minimal standards for employment of pastoral staff. CPE was a part of those requirements. In the specialized ministry of prison chaplaincy, the essentials of a CPE experience contributed two indispensable factors to the pastor's competencies: 1) a need to know the personality structure of individual inmates, and 2) the development of the chaplain's confidence to know him/herself well enough to engage in one-on-one counseling with the prisoner. Successful ministry was measured in therapeutic terms. There was a time period when employment for Protestants in many state prison systems was dependent on having CPE credentials, even though many practitioners were convinced that the value of the experience varied greatly depending on the individual student and/or clinical supervisor. Some also questioned how effectively the field experiences gained in one institutional setting—a hospital, for example—might apply to workplace encounters within a different institutional environment—such as a prison.

Endemic to the professional development of chaplaincy along clinical lines was a commitment to the *medical model* associated with the rehabilitative ideal fostered by scientific positivism. Given this underlying notion and the reliance on the CPE ministry model, the preferred title for this new professional soon became *Clinical Chaplain*, a term that depicted the religio-psychosocial correctional specialist many chaplains had become. Thus, when in the 1970s some correctional administrators began to question the value of chaplaincy services, chaplains were quick to defend their existence on the basis of their clinical skill sets rather than their theologically based pastoral preparation.

But the dynamism of change continued. Serious and broad-based demand for the accommodation of religious needs of the contemporary prison population began in the late 1980s and early 1990s. Congress and the Attorney Generals consistently pressured publicly funded institutions to be more inclusive in every way and through every means available—all genders, racial and ethnic distinctions, and all faiths. Institutions had to comply with a myriad of new federal guidelines that attempted to ensure equal opportunity for all Americans. It was the litany of the land, and it applied to prisons and—in a more oblique way—to prisoners.

The choice to believe or not to believe was established as an absolute right of prisoners. They also had the right to litigate and had free access to the courts, which they readily exercised. Soon after the right to believe in a religion as a choice was defined, prisoners asserted the assumed right to free and full practice of all those attendant issues of religion. The courts agreed, and the rather rudimentary trio of Protestant, Jewish, and Catholic quickly mushroomed into dozens of additional faith groups who demanded, and usually received, equal opportunity to observe and practice the fundamentals of their faith.

Concurrent with this faith group expansion was a time of rapid increase in prison population and construction in America without equal in the history of corrections. What Schlosser labeled as the "Correctional Industrial Complex" became firmly entrenched during these years of unparalleled growth (see Schlosser).

Spartan-like institutions were built, with an eye toward economy of operation and management, which had a negative impact on both religious space allocation and staffing patterns. In the first place, the multipurpose space became a standard of construction design, replacing the designated chapel with its religious education rooms and professionally styled office space. Moreover, this new space was usually less central to the stream of inmate traffic than traditional chapel placement had been. Second, budgetary constraints identified traditional staffing patterns into two easily discernible categories—the essential (security) and the nonessential (various program functions in which chaplaincy was always included). In such an environment, chaplains were easily identified as expendable personnel.

Perhaps no area of correctional change has been more pronounced than the religious arena. At a time when resources were diminishing, an expanded cultural, racial, and religiously diverse inmate population placed new demands on prison systems. Both federal and state correctional systems underwent a metamorphosis in an effort to provide for all faiths now present in significant numbers and demanding accommodation. Chaplains felt the pressures of this change as well. The result was that they, too, refashioned themselves, yet again, in a way that both responded to inmate religious needs and enhanced the value of the profession. They became managers—facilitators of religious activities.

This new role demanded not only a different set of skills, but also a new positioning within the prison. Just as earlier notions of "pastoring" had shifted from the model of shepherd to that of clinician, now many chaplains abandoned roles of faith representation to position themselves as neutral conduits through which any and all faiths might flow. Institutional administrators, on the other hand, began to look to chaplains as quasi-legal experts in the faith practices of all recognized religions—a role that chaplains readily embraced. Once again, new titles were created, most often incorporating the term "religious" (to delineate the multiple-faith job emphasis) and/or "coordinator" (to clearly distinguish the position as a facilitator, rather than a deliverer of services).

The transition from the delivery of primarily Christian services to facilitation of interfaith practices dovetailed with another emerging reality of the profession, which was the lack of candidates from non-Christian groups who both aspired to serve in correctional chaplaincy and who also met the hiring qualifications imposed by many systems. The available pool of chaplains had traditionally consisted of largely white, male, and either Protestant, Roman Catholic, or in fewer numbers, Jewish clergy. By the 1990s, the number of Catholic priests had diminished worldwide, few Islamic clergy (Imams) had been either identified or recruited, and Jewish rabbis were rarely available for full-time employment in correctional systems. Smaller religious groups had even fewer identifiable leaders. Rather quickly, the demand exceeded the supply in every area except the ranks of Protestant chaplains.

More recently, efforts by the ACCA leadership to establish widely accepted specific standards for certifying the credentials of correctional chaplains have been largely unfulfilled, even though that organization is the officially recognized affiliate of the ACA. Individual states have continued to set their own qualifications for hiring chaplains, as well as for determining how chaplains are incorporated into departmental superstructures. Nor has the primary distinguishing training credential, Clinical Pastoral Education, maintained its primacy. In the current market, CPE is no longer viewed as an absolute credential for entrance into chaplaincy and "equivalencies" have become increasingly more acceptable. Perhaps more significantly, while professional chaplains have encouraged minimum standards for education, experience, and clinical training components, they have paid little attention to issues of competency. There are simply no broadly accepted criteria to demonstrate effectiveness of chaplaincy role function.

The result is that systems vary widely in their hiring patterns for chaplaincy positions. Some states not only don't employ chaplains, they don't even recognize such a staff position, voluntary or otherwise (e.g., South Dakota). Instead, they merely offer religious services to inmates that are supplied by community religious leaders. Several states contract for all chaplaincy services (e.g., Georgia); others use a combination of full-time employees and contracted personnel (e.g., Maryland). At least one state that employs no chaplains uses a sole-service provider (Virginia), while others (e.g., Colorado) utilize more than one private faith-based provider. Educational and experiential requirements also fluctuate a great deal from system to system. While a significant percentage of states specify no minimal educational requirements, the norm is at least an undergraduate degree. Nearly one-third require graduate degrees. Often, some sort of supervised ministry experience is required, and almost all systems look for some evidence of previous pastoral ministry experience.

> *The clear trend for entry positions has been toward fewer academic absolutes, either with respect to degrees or specific courses; fewer nonnegotiable clinical experiences; and almost no uniform expectations across faith traditions.*

A 2002 survey I conducted cataloged responses from departments of corrections in 39 states and the Bureau of Prisons that detailed each agency's minimal hiring requirements for entry-level chaplains (see Appendix 1). At that time, four states had no publically funded chaplains. Of the remaining 35 states, 9 had no formal educational requirements, 15 required an undergraduate degree, and 11 asked for a master's degree. Only 16 states required varying numbers of CPE units, most of whom would accept some sort of equivalent as a replacement, thereby fulfilling *ACA Standards* requirements. This survey data clearly demonstrated that even at that point in time, there were no widespread agreed-upon educational qualifications or accepted preparation for professional correctional chaplains across the nation. In the middle part of that decade, the ACCA made an intense, but unsuccessful effort to embed increased minimal qualifications into the *ACA Standards*.

The clear trend for entry positions has been toward fewer academic absolutes, either with respect to degrees or specific courses; fewer nonnegotiable clinical experiences; and almost no uniform expectations across faith traditions. Some systems have migrated to a more easily defensible position of demanding no credentials beyond what a specific denomination or faith group declares to be adequate for a clergy person of that faith. Those systems are unlikely to be influenced by outside sources of standards, whether academic, specialized training, or any experiential-based service that cannot be directly tied to performance.

Our discussion, thus far, has focused entirely on prisons—and for a good reason. For the most part, chaplains serving county or regional jails have been only marginally influenced by their prison counterparts. Jails are locally operated institutions. In the case of a county facility, they are supervised by that county's sheriff or designee; multicounty boards provide oversight for regional jails. In either case, they are worlds of their own, not parts of a larger systemic network, and thus the local managing entity makes its own rules concerning chaplaincy staff, which means there is a huge variation in chaplaincy services between institutions.

By far, the norm within these facilities is to have a volunteer from the community designated as the "official" chaplain who coordinates programs and whatever individual counseling is deemed necessary. In the case of smaller jails, it is not uncommon for the designated jail administrator—often a uniformed correctional staff member—to oversee these services, all of which are delivered by a pool of community volunteers. In larger jail settings, there is more often a nonprofit jail ministry, usually locally organized and supported, which handles chaplaincy services for the facility or—in the case of mega-jails—multiple nonprofit providers. These organizations employ the chaplain who then functions as unpaid staff, reporting to both the Jail Administrator or Sheriff and the local supporting entity. There are a limited number of nonprofits who place chaplains in multiple institutions—*Good News Jail & Prison Ministry*, headquartered in Richmond, Virginia, is the largest of these, with chaplains currently employed in 22 states.

> *Having transitioned from the role of preacher-of-salvation to that of rehabilitative clinician and eventually to manager-facilitator and quasi-legal expert, chaplains now find themselves struggling to locate a transcendent core identity that can sustain them in the midst of perpetual systemic changes.*

In this sort of environment, not only does the breadth and scope of pastoral delivery vary, but so does the quality. In short, lacking any systemic philosophy, direction, or accountability, jail chaplains often function at marginally acceptable levels. Although an institution may be able to claim compliance with minimal constitutional guarantees, relatively few jails offer substantive chaplaincy services. However, exceptions to this general rule are growing in number, thanks in large part to recent efforts by leadership within the American Jail Association (AJA) which have begun to highlight the quagmire of legal issues surrounding religious rights of prisoners.

Still missing from the emerging dialogue, however, are any discussions about what a fully orbed chaplaincy services program might look like and what expectations should be established for the staff chaplain overseeing its delivery. The theoretical principles and specific processes laid out in the chapters that follow apply equally to both jail and prison chaplains. Where the differing environments and missions of the two create a need for distinctive approaches, we will identify the variations and discuss both in detail. Far too little has been written about jail chaplaincy; this text may serve as a beginning remedy to that.

Meanwhile, change continues, unabated, in prison and jail chaplaincy: the ongoing expansion of services to include more faith practices; adjustments of required entry-level credentials; the quest to measure effectiveness of chaplains; and variations of acceptable paradigms for providing religious services for prisoners. Having transitioned from the role of preacher-of-salvation to that of rehabilitative clinician and eventually to manager-facilitator and quasi-legal expert, chaplains now find themselves struggling to locate a transcendent core identity that can sustain them in the midst of perpetual systemic changes. In addition, they are being pressured by the systems in which they work to justify their presence in some measurable way. In an era of ongoing budgetary reductions, an elusive job description, along with the absence of measurable performance indicators place chaplains at risk in many state systems.

In the face of these challenges, the ACCA leadership has aggressively campaigned to establish what they consider the nonnegotiables of service as a correctional chaplain. In doing so, they have chosen a distinctive phrase to describe those who belong to some acceptable core of chaplains—"qualified professional" (*ACA Standards* use the term "qualified chaplain"). "Qualified" clearly refers to training and preparation; what the word "professional" means is less clear. However, in all their communications, the

ACCA implies that a proven training agenda and preferred credentialing process exists that ensures professional functionality.

But such is not the case. First, there are almost no structured chaplaincy programs available in American universities and seminaries. The ones that exist usually offer a generic institutional focus through a course that incorporates military, health care, workplace, first responder and a variety of other chaplaincy roles in addition to correctional chaplaincy, and then allow the student to gain practicum credit through a field placement or internship. (For an example of a text that accompanies such a course, see Paget, Naomi K. and Janet R. McCormick, *The Work of the Chaplain*. Valley Forge, PA: Judson Press, 2006.) It is extremely rare to find even one course dedicated to correctional ministry, and pastoral counseling courses spend little time considering life issues of a clientele that reflects any similarity to the profiles of those individuals chaplains encounter in correctional institutions. The normal preparation for any chaplain is an education in the tenets of the chaplain's faith group. For Christians, this would mean theological training at an accredited institution. In addition, while approximately half of the states require an employed chaplain to have some units of Clinical Pastoral Education or an equivalency, this experience is seldom structured around ministry in a correctional setting. Most often, a hospital serves as the field site, and the CPE Supervisor almost never has corrections experience. Thus, few agency-funded chaplains come to their initial position with any corrections-focused training in advance. It's just not available. Always, chaplains are highly dependent on their on-the-job experiences, limited mentoring from other colleagues, in-service training opportunities, and whatever corollary continuing education offerings they can find after they are already placed.

The term "qualified" may refer to an ideal model suggested by the ACCA or other group, but there is no agreement as to what it means among individual state departments of corrections. Nor does any study exist that demonstrates any differentiation between the quality of chaplaincy services delivered based on these varying levels of requirements. Interestingly, any requirement that demands a graduate seminary degree only accentuates an existing bias toward mainline Protestant denominations that dates from our mid-century proscribed formulas. The pathway to ministry licensure or ordination for many Christian denominations is a four-year college degree, but preparation for either the Catholic priesthood or Islamic faith leadership is not identical to this long-standing requirement. Recognition of this fact in the current era has led to the more frequent acceptance of educational equivalencies for non-Christian chaplains, though the minimal standard for Protestant chaplains has remained more rigorous.

At the heart of the concerns about professionalism is the notion that lesser prepared chaplains are unable to accommodate religious diversity by effectively coordinating the various activities of the broad range of faith groups now active within correctional settings in a manner that "assures equal status and protection for all religions" (*ACCA Standard 4–4512*). Without question, the unique demands of the correctional setting requires—in addition to a thorough knowledge of Scripture—a special skill set that includes highly polished counseling skills, strong management and facilitation abilities, a working knowledge of various faith group requirements, adequate understanding of constitutional law as it pertains to faith practices in the institution, and a strong commitment to serving all residents of the institution regardless of their faith identity or lack thereof.

However, only the last of these—which is essentially a heart issue—can generally be obtained outside the immediate context of a correctional setting. Academic religious institutions very seldom teach anything about legal matters within institutional settings, unless they offer an actual course in chaplaincy, which few do. Although some sort of exposure to world religions is usually available, it is not always required, and exposure to one generalized course on the topic is still not adequate preparation for the careful facilitation of the various faiths active inside jails and prisons. Moreover, rarely—if ever—do classes in religious institutions of higher learning focus on complex criminal behaviors, the sociopathies that accompany incarceration, or the family dynamics that are the normative experiences in the lives of inmates that chaplains counsel on a regular basis. Finally, the managerial skills essential to overseeing the myriad of chaplaincy services offered within a sophisticated institutional structure are not taught in the religious academic setting.

The unique blend of knowledge, skills, abilities, and heart is simply not obtained in one localized institution or through a single educational experience. Newly hired chaplains come to their position with little directly applicable training. The fortunate few are mentored by an experienced colleague (that opportunity has rapidly dwindled in the face of diminished funding for positions), but the vast majority develop their expertise through the crucible of ongoing engagement with the staff and inmates who populate the unique world of the jail or prison they serve. Newly appointed chaplains are rarely prepared in advance for the work they are about to undertake so, by definition, they are unqualified when they assume their initial placement.

There remains one final matter that is considered by some to be crucial to chaplaincy professionalism—the question of who employs the chaplain. Since the requirement of "free exercise" is a constitutional requirement, some feel that only a government employee can effectively monitor the interests of the state. Furthermore, they extend that argument to state that anyone who receives their funding from an alternative source—a church denomination, a nonprofit, or any other sending body—owes allegiance to that body to such a degree that those interests impair their ability to deliver services to groups outside their personal faith tradition and leads them to promote the tenants of their particular faith group.

In a speech delivered at the 2007 American Correctional Association Congress, Dr. Vance Drum, a seasoned Texas chaplain, articulated this position. Though in the written version of this talk, he offers the disclaimer that his views do not necessarily represent the views of any other association to which he belongs, they do closely parallel arguments made by other members of the ACCA—both verbal and written—at other times and places. That organization's website also provides a link to Drum's speech, which suggests support for his remarks. After emphasizing the crucial need for chaplains to provide for the religious needs of incarcerated individuals outside their own faith group, Drum says this:

> The constitutional requirement of "free exercise" is a state requirement and, in my view, one which is best ensured and safeguarded by an employee of the state. Volunteer, or specific faith chaplains who are compensated by their faith group, provide valuable and necessary ministry. However, it is my conviction that, by virtue of their faith-group-originated compensation, they would normally have a fiduciary obligation, or

a contractual obligation, to especially promote the interests of their particular faith group. As we say in Texas, you dance with the one that brung you, and you look out for the one who pays you. Professional, state-supplied chaplains have no such obligation to promote the interests of one faith group over another. In fact, the obligation is the opposite—to treat all the faith groups without favoritism. (Drum 2007)

This position is problematic in several ways. For one thing, all chaplains—even those employed by governmental agencies—must have ecclesiastical endorsement from some organization, usually their respective denominational headquarters or sending agency. These affiliations carry their own expectations of the chaplains that are distinct from and sometimes inconsistent with those of the correctional system where the chaplain serves. In most cases, too, that sending agency must periodically renew their endorsement of the chaplain's correctional placement. But such a duality of expectation and authority lines do not disqualify or necessarily hinder the chaplains' institutional work.

> *A critical question facing chaplaincy in the coming era is:* **What is it that a chaplain does that no one else in the correctional facility can?** *To overemphasize the role of facilitator-manager or legal expert whose primary role is to keep the state free of constitutional liabilities at the expense of the pastoral functions is a dangerous strategy that places the chaplain's birthright in jeopardy.*

More importantly, the premise that any "specific faith" leader is automatically unable to perform without bias is both unfair and unsupportable. There have been and continue to be many nongovernmental chaplains who serve their facilities and inmate populations in full accordance with RLUIPA and RFRA guidelines and institutional processes. They faithfully render unto Caesar what is his, and to God what belongs to Him. That not everyone is able to function this way is true. Navigating these difficult waters as one who represents transcendent values while at the same time working within a carefully structured legal environment is part of that unique framework within which all correctional chaplains must work. But there are also cases where government-employed chaplains are unable to effectively work within appropriate boundaries of the model and must be disciplined accordingly. The problem is not contained by merely controlling the source of the paycheck.

Although Dr. Drum sees nothing wrong with the chaplain dancing with the state, that relationship does give rise to another problem—one that has clearly impacted the state of chaplaincy in America. Placing undo emphasis on the constitutionally-based tasks of the chaplain's position has narrowed the field of vision, and in some instances, reduced the position to that of "keeper of the law" rather than "keeper of the cloak." The result is that in some states—Missouri and Idaho are examples—chaplaincy positions have been discarded in favor of *Religious Activities Coordinators*. After all, if the primary function of the chaplain is to safeguard the interests of the state, that fact surely diminishes the value in that employee's pastoral role. It also raises the question of whether or not that person even needs pastoral credentials.

Whatever the source of financial support, chaplains must clearly demonstrate a value to the correctional facility beyond that of constitutional watchdog. A critical question facing chaplaincy in the coming era is: *What is it that a chaplain does that no one else in the correctional facility can?* To overemphasize the role of facilitator-manager or legal expert whose primary role is to keep the state free of constitutional liabilities at the expense of the pastoral functions is a dangerous strategy that places the chaplain's birthright in jeopardy.

Serving professionally is an issue of functional competence, and it flows organically from those who understand the unique territory of institutional ministry, have a full commitment to concepts of chaplaincy, and are both well-trained and effectively mentored. One thing nearly everyone agrees on is that any jail or prison administration striving for a healthy spiritual component and the accrued values that such a program delivers needs to have a dedicated position—staffed by a competent chaplain—overseeing delivery of a wide-ranging set of chaplaincy services. What seems to be missing is a quality control process that delivers both personal competency and any institutional program paradigm with great consistency. The profession of correctional chaplaincy lacks:

- A broadly accepted set of theoretical core principles
- Any clear preparatory route for emerging personnel
- A set of agreed-upon functional performance standards (*ACA Standards* are largely process and policy-oriented rather than outcomes-based)
- Job-related continuing education opportunities

Professionalism can neither be assumed nor assured by virtue of an appointment to a position; nor can it be derived from academic preparation alone. Being called a chaplain won't make you one, and education alone does not equate to professional competency. Professionalism is functional—the consistent delivery of a set of appropriate tasks with excellence. Correctional chaplaincy must develop evaluative measures that are complementary with the broad variety of tasks the job entails, and confidence in credentials (what one brings to the job) must yield to performance outcomes (how effectively one functions). What follows in the balance of this book is a first step toward meeting at least a portion of these needs.

*A portion of this chapter previously appeared in Beckner, W. Thomas and Charles R. Riggs. 2002. *A View of a New Paradigm in Prison Chaplaincy.* Fort Wayne, IN: Center for Justice and Urban Leadership, Taylor University.

REFERENCES

American Chaplaincy Training School. (2002). Unpublished report. Survey of state correctional agencies.

Drum, Vance L. Professional Chaplaincy: Fact and Fiction. Speech delivered at the *American Correctional Association Congress*, Kansas City, MO, August 13, 2007.

Friedman, Gary. Email communication with the author, May 28, 2008.

Paget, Naomi K. and Janet R. McCormick. (2006). *The Work of the Chaplain*. Valley Forge, PA: Judson Press.

Schlosser, Eric. (1998). The Prison-Industrial Complex. *Atlantic Monthly*, December, 51–77.

Skotnicki, Andrew. (2000). *Religion and the Development of the American Penal System*. Lanham, MD: University Press of America.

Chapter Three

Searching for a Meaningful Chaplaincy Paradigm

T he profession of correctional chaplaincy suffers from a lack of any significant body of literature. Historically, chaplains have written little about their profession, and for the most part, few academicians have demonstrated any serious interest in this field of inquiry. To be sure, in recent years much has been written about prison and jail "ministry" as viewed by volunteer ministers or leaders of nonprofit organizations who approach correctional settings as mission fields. None of those writings examines the role of chaplain in any depth, focusing instead on the delivery of volunteer ministry services by outside agents. Most of the remaining literature offers either only anecdotal evidence of the chaplain's accomplishments or presents superficial explorations of selected pastoral functions. Only a handful of studies provide any in-depth analysis of the chaplaincy.

Seminal to any exploration of the professional chaplain is Dale Pace's 1976 study (Pace). The book's title, *A Christian's Guide to Effective Jail & Prison Ministries*, is misleading; the book is in fact a study of correctional chaplaincy. Though dated in some ways, much of the book remains remarkably current and should be read by every chaplain for its comprehensive overview of the profession, clear delineation of critical issues that define tensions within the field that remain even today, and for its research-based approach to chaplaincy praxis.

Pace outlined the evolving nature of chaplaincy in the twentieth century and correctly identified a shift in emphasis away from the counseling role to that of program coordination, a trend that at that time was still embryonic. He also discerned that a significant driving force of that movement was the heightened concern with inmate rights by the courts of the land and first articulated what has since become axiomatic:

> Inmates have the right to the religion of their choice (including no religion). Furthermore, the state cannot support or promote one religious persuasion over another. Thus, logically, the chaplain (as a state employee in many cases) runs the risk of putting the state in the position of promoting a religion if he does not promote *all* religious programs equally, that is, become a "broker" for all faith groups. . . . government chaplains will be forced by future court decisions to move more and more into the role of religious program coordinator. (79–80)

Denominations support and reinforce bible college and seminary programs that for the most part ignore correctional ministry; thus those schools produce pastors and other leaders who are seldom sensitive to the need for such ministry, and therefore, fail to encourage outreach to prisoners or their families within their congregations.

Pace inserts a perceptive footnote at this point that illustrates just how relevant his work remains, 35 years after it was written: "A related question that may come to the front is, Does the 'religious program coordinator' need to be a minister if his role is essentially administrative? This author sees no reason a religious program coordinator must be a minister" (271). Indeed, as we mentioned in the previous chapter, this question remains a critical item in the current chaplaincy environment. At the same time, Pace speculated that a likely development would be that interest groups would someday challenge the legitimacy of government-supported chaplains, resulting in judicial rulings declaring their employment a violation of the separation of church and state. Thus far, that prophecy has not proven valid, though administrators in at least one state—Colorado—have used similar reasoning to support their replacement of paid chaplains with unpaid and/ or privately funded staff chaplains.

A Christian's Guide to Effective Jail & Prison Ministries also identified some critical systemic problems that continue to stymie the growth of the profession to this day. First, the Church fails to honor the men and women who serve in correctional chaplaincy to the same degree that they do those who minister in congregational settings (41). Denominations support and reinforce bible college and seminary programs that for the most part ignore correctional ministry; thus those schools produce pastors and other leaders who are seldom sensitive to the need for such ministry, and therefore, fail to encourage outreach to prisoners or their families within their congregations. In turn, those congregations support educational institutions and ministry models that reproduce more of what they, themselves, resemble.

And the cycle continues. There are still few prophetic voices calling the Church to a work among the incarcerated. Pace also pointed out the lack of institutionally focused chaplaincy training made available either in the Church's formal educational settings or the arena of continuing educational opportunities (132).

Finally, Pace challenged two levels of standards for chaplains that have not yet been adequately addressed: 1) the appropriate standard for entrance into chaplaincy; and 2) the demonstration of professional competency (133–37). Certainly, these two factors are highly interactive. In every profession, an attempt is made to prepare people in such a way that they are then able to effectively deliver the competencies required of them; at any point where the two fail to be aligned, a breakdown occurs. Moreover, preparation and competency intersect with the cluster of specific tasks that comprise the correctional chaplain's job. Therefore, only when we clearly delineate the chaplain's institutional roles are we able to discern both the outcomes required and the preparation necessary to accomplish them. The major portion of this text addresses this intersection and the interrelatedness of these components.

Here, too, Pace broke essential ground with his examination of the "contemporary praxis of correctional chaplaincy," based on a survey of 172 full-time chaplains who reported on their time use and the activities they supervised. His respondents included both Catholic and Protestant chaplains serving jails, federal and state prisons, and juvenile facilities. Not content with this merely descriptive profile, he then attempted to correlate the data to evaluate the impact of eight parameters on the individual chaplain's ministry: 1) theological persuasion, 2) denominational affiliation, 3) level of academic education, 4) CPE training, 5) type of institution served, 6) employer (church or state), 7) facilities for ministry within the institution, and 8) prior parish experience (87–105).

Although the intention was noble, the task was difficult, and Pace's interpretations remain controversial. He claimed that "evangelical" chaplains are more successful in ministry to offenders than their "liberal" peers (95–97); that offenders also respond more poorly to CPE–trained chaplains (100–01); and that privately funded chaplains worked longer hours, were more engaged with religious activities, and had difficulty identifying their personal theological positioning (103–04). Elsewhere in the volume, he expands his criticism of CPE's effectiveness (143–45), and in a debate on the merits of government-paid chaplaincies, clearly favors a Church-supported model.

Inexcusably, none of the more recent academic explorations of chaplaincy have referenced Pace's groundbreaking work. Whether one agrees with Pace's conclusions or not, his effort to apply a research paradigm to correctional chaplaincy was a pioneering venture—one that has been only partially replicated in the years since. There remains little supportable data from which any substantial conclusions can be drawn about the work of chaplaincy in the jails and prisons of our land.

Henry G. Covert's *Ministry to the Incarcerated* provides valuable insights into the pastoral dimension of the chaplain's work. First, he accurately points out that the context within which chaplains work is unlike that of most pastoral counselors, noting that according to the Psychosocial Stressor Scale in the *DSM-III-R* most incarcerated individuals would be evaluated as undergoing "enduring stress". He then notes the connection between stress and the depression that often results from continued stress.

> Depression is evident in correctional facilities, often destroying inmate advancements and potential. Having lost their enthusiasm, perspective, and hope, some felons withdraw into their own world of cynicism. Anger and aggressive behavior also indicates chronic depression. These moods affect the entire institution, leaving the lingering possibility for conflict. (16)

Of course, the inmates bring their own particular psychological and behavioral dysfunctions to the institution, filtered through—in most cases—years of negative interactions with their free-world environment. Then, they are forced to coexist in confined quarters and adhere to institutional structures and rules that often destroy what little dignity they have left. This only increases the level of stress.

> Correctional facilities are molded by the clashes of races, cultures, and religions, where prisoners compete for power, control, and survival. They are neighborhoods of discontent where anxiety and fear translate into mistrust and manipulation. As communities separated from society, prisons function apart from the rapidly changing world and this environment affects tension levels. (17)

Dr. Covert goes on to identify a lengthy list of specific inmate stressors, all of which frame a unique and highly complex ministry environment. Some of the stressors include issues the prisoner brings with him in to the facility—e.g., low self-esteem, personal guilt, unresolved anger, unrealistic expectations—which are then exacerbated by the prison culture. Other stressors have to do with the physical or structural restrictions that are embedded characteristics of any correctional institution—visitation rules, mail and phone regulations, medical care, and similar matters. The majority of the stressors, however, are those unique to the correctional environment but to which inmates adjust with a high degree of variation. Prison living conditions force a large number of highly diverse and undersocialized people together in confined spaces where they must interact civilly with each other and with staff whose role it is to manage and control a multitude of individual inmate behaviors. At the same time, most inmates are busy absorbing a series of personal losses: economic loss; loss of free will and control over even the simplest of activities; loss of relationships with those most dear to them; loss of sexual intimacy, etc. (20–63). Covert analyzes these and other pastoral issues from the vantage point of a seasoned chaplain, while interweaving substantial research from related academic disciplines. The result is a useful overview of contextual ministry within the correctional setting.

What becomes clear to the observant reader through this presentation is that the pastoral role of the correctional chaplain is unlike any other. A jail or prison does not, in any significant way, resemble a free-world parish. Seminary courses don't provide adequate preparation for a ministry to offenders residing in correctional institutions. Neither is a jail or prison similar to a hospital; the physical impairments of patients and the mission of medical staff are hardly equal to their correctional counterparts. For that reason, clinical pastoral experience gained within a medical facility is of only limited value to a newly placed correctional chaplain.

Having considered the pastoral contexts of chaplaincy, Covert then introduces three distinct paradigms for institutional ministry—models he believes are especially capable of addressing the feelings and beliefs of inmates within their unique cultural setting. The first of these is *the dimensions of the cross.*

> Through the example of Christ at Calvary prisoners see a savior who experienced the legal system of his day. They follow the events that occurred after our Lord's arrest and, although his imprisonment was brief, see that Christ is like them. Prisoners are drawn to a God who can truly identify with their plight. They can relate to a savior who understands their feelings of isolation and abandonment. Inmates gravitate toward Jesus because he knows the pain of being misunderstood, rejected by humanity, and seemingly forgotten by God. (71)

In his discussion on this point, Covert stresses the depths of love, the cost of forgiveness, the need for grace, and Christ's advocacy on behalf of sinners. This theology "does not promise easy victories or offer false security. Rather, it promises grace from a savior who relates to humanity through his own wounds. It also promises victory over sin, struggle, and death" (76).

In the midst of experiencing feelings of isolation and abandonment within a correctional facility, inmates need *the ministry of presence*, Covert's second ministry paradigm. Contrasting Job's friends who thought they were engaging in ministry but who were actually making matters worse, Covert provides what might well be a functional summation of the work of chaplaincy: "The caring presence of another person during a time of trial can be healing. In a mysterious way, sharing our burdens with another person brings relief. Two people can form an emotional bond when the compassion is void of insensitive advice, theological rhetoric, criticism, and judgment" (79).

Covert's final paradigm is *the priesthood of servants*. In a rich theological exploration of this topic, he presents a vivid model for an active church behind bars with its inmate members both serving and being served by one another. Noting that inmates usually see themselves as needy and useless, Covert emphasizes the significance of their participatory role in the body of incarcerated believers.

> The priesthood brings renewed life to prison ministry and the inmate community. The numerous needs of offenders, combined with the limitations placed on clergy, make the priesthood indispensable in prison. It transforms a lifeless structure into an organism that lives and moves through the power of the Holy Spirit. Through the priesthood inmates can experience a fellowship of love and mutual support. (89)

This is a critical principle for chaplains to understand. Inmates must move beyond seeing themselves as victims and ongoing recipients of services; they must work through their personal pain and turn their eyes outward to the needs of others; and they must grasp the importance of koinonia as an instrument of grace. Covert articulates an axiom every chaplain should embrace: "Any ministry that only addresses individuals without emphasizing the need for community nurturing and mutual healing will never be strong and in time it will fade away" (91).

Ministry to the Incarcerated stands alone as an in-depth theological excursion into the pastoral roles of correctional chaplaincy. Though it considers the psychological and sociological dynamics at work in the lives of offenders, especially as they play out inside jails and prisons, it focuses on the spiritual dimension of their lives within that unique cultural setting, and its lens is consistently that of the chaplain. Dr. Covert has made a significant contribution to the body of chaplaincy literature.

Published the same year—1995—was a work by Rev. Richard Denis Shaw—*Chaplains to the Imprisoned: Sharing Life with the Incarcerated*—that was fashioned from his 1990 doctoral dissertation. Having discovered a paucity of literature describing the function of the profession in his own research, the author's stated goal for this book was to offer a "portrait of chaplaincy" (2). Like any portrait, the image created bears the distinct imprint of its creator; Shaw's text is an amalgam of quantitative research, socio-political perspectives, and personal reflections based on more than two decades of chaplaincy experiences. The final product offers unique insights of great merit intermingled with strongly opinionated declarations about the appropriate identity of the correctional chaplain and his/her interactions with administrative officials within correctional facilities.

For his research, Shaw formulated a questionnaire that focused on the stress factors associated with the chaplaincy in three dimensions of their job: 1) the demands of ministering in a correctional facility; 2) the pressures of serving in a setting where great demands are placed on relationships; and 3) strategies for coping with these inherent stresses and demands (163). In examining the first two dimensions, Shaw asked the chaplains to scale their responses to a list of facility stressors and relational demands according to the frequency and intensity of the listed item, using a five-point Likert Scale. He then coded the responses to differentiate between the nature of the facility served, its security designation, and certain personal characteristics of the chaplain-respondent. While most, though not all, of the questions could be technically classified as "open-ended," a significant majority presented a clearly distinguished bias of the writer, a methodological tendency that damages the validity of the instrument from a social science research perspective (see 160–63).

Shaw confined his initial mailing to chaplains within his own state (New York), and it was this sample that was used in his original doctoral dissertation. Later, he was able to obtain additional responses from the majority of Federal Bureau of Prison chaplains that, he concludes, substantiate the findings of his first inquiry. Though Shaw avers that incorporating these data from additional respondents nullifies the obvious skewing of his original population (19), the narrowness of the study cannot be overlooked. Nor can the fact that of the 183 chaplains surveyed, only 13 served county or city jails be overlooked. Moreover, as constructed, Shaw's study offers a limited view of the chaplain's total function; it dwells entirely on a set of negatively stated stressors rather than attempting any comprehensive overview of the position.

> *For chaplains, stress begins with the feeling that they are isolated from the religious mainstream where neither the government whom they serve nor the churches they represent respect their work or appear to be supportive of it.*

Nonetheless, the strength of this book lies in the "voice" it gives to chaplains who daily serve their institutions, coping with those stressors that comprise the very warp and woof of their ministries. Its value rests in the qualitative rather than quantitative measures, and the authentic perceptions of the chaplains surveyed add valuable context for our exploration of the chaplain's functional role, even if their voices reflect mostly negatively stated feelings about their work.

For chaplains, stress begins with the feeling that they are isolated from the religious mainstream where neither the government whom they serve nor the churches they represent respect their work or appear to be supportive of it. This dual loyalty—serving the state while at the same time honoring the transcendent authority of God—often leads to conflicts with correctional administrators who reject such a position (66–69). (Early commentaries written by chaplains nearly always emphasize this conflict, something that has largely disappeared from discussions of the refashioned roles we described in Chapter Two). Chaplains describe the difficulties of working with correctional officers and other professional staff members. At the heart of this issue seems to be the minimalization of the chaplain's credentials, a point Shaw effectively challenges.

Much of the literature seems to assume that the quality of the chaplain is a variable (owing to personality, professional training, or theological outlook) while the quality of the professional staff is a constant. Not only are most professional staff members in correctional facilities overwhelmed by the sheer numbers of clients they must deal with, as individuals they are as variable in quality as any chaplains. (77)

Chaplains also must deal with a public who seldom understand or appreciate their role, both the conservative citizens who possess simplistic attitudes about crime and punishment and the political activists whose agenda is to reform the justice system. Both, in their own way, denigrate the role of the chaplain who works within the system (79).

The chaplain-respondents also deal with internal conflicts within their own ranks. While Shaw sees chaplains of mainline denominations tending to work together within the facilities, a trend that reflects the movement within the larger community, he finds that a clear chasm exists between some groups.

Professional cooperation between mainline Christian churches, however, accentuates a division which has always existed within the wide spectrum of Protestant denominations, and which now exists with Protestants and Catholics on one side, representing the denominations willing to mix religion with the sciences, and fundamentalist denominations on the other side, in general relying only upon the Bible as a guide to living and scorning any sort of wedding between professionalism and religion. (82)

But Shaw fails to recognize any points along a continuum between "mainline" and "fundamentalist", a failure that mars some of his conclusions. Nonetheless, he does correctly identify this tension that underlies a group of stressors he discusses in the pages that follow: ministry delivery methods, use and value of volunteer groups, and what he labels "do-it-yourself religion" (83–87).

In a chapter entitled "Sharing Life with the Incarcerated", Shaw discusses those relational stressors inherent to the position of chaplain.

The highest intensity ratings were assigned to the following categories: *overcrowding, and the subsequent overloading of ministerial responsibilities; frustration about observed injustices within the criminal justice system; dealing with inmates' family crises; and lack of rehabilitative impact of their ministry.* More moderately rated items included *dealing with mentally ill inmates who should be in hospitals rather than in prisons; hearing the same old stories over and over, told by inmates who fit very predictable patterns of behavior;* and *being conned* (122–23). Shaw's commentary on the social chasm that exists between chaplains and inmates and the ways in which it influences pastoral engagements is especially perceptive (112–15). Despite the seriousness of these stressors, chaplains in Shaw's study disagree that the conditions create burnout: "Most chaplains acknowledged the presence of factors in their work which might cause stress, but at the same time they made it clear that they felt themselves capable of coping with these realities. Many of them refer to a mellowing, observed within themselves over time" (121). The careful reader is left to wonder how, precisely, this mellowing is reflected in the chaplain's day-to-day ministry.

The overall portrait of chaplaincy that emerges from Shaw's work is that of dedicated chaplains, working primarily in isolation within their professional lives and in relation to their religious affiliate groups. They tend to be at odds with administrative goals of their particular institutions, yet nonetheless play crucial roles in providing some sense of balance and healthy spirituality within a broken and sometimes abusive correctional system. Underappreciated and not given the status they deserve, those who survive and flourish are the resilient ones who creatively manage the inherent stresses of the position. While Shaw often overstates his case and seems intent on illustrating the polarities within the work environment, there is a great deal to glean from the material in his book. The voices of the many chaplains represented provide a sense of texture and context of chaplaincy that is unavailable elsewhere in the professional literature.

Interestingly, it is academicians rather than professional chaplains who have done the most to objectively illuminate the wide range of duties associated with this position and to explore the ways in which those tasks intersect. Jody L. Sundt and Francis T. Cullen, in a series of discrete yet related studies between 1998 and 2007 have provided a body of data from which we can begin to create a useful paradigm. *"The Role of the Contemporary Prison Chaplain"* (1998) uses the results of a national sample of 232 chaplains to investigate 1) the breadth of the chaplain's role, both secular and spiritual activities; 2) the extent to which those roles primarily serve either rehabilitative or custodial purposes; and 3) the degree of role conflict that chaplains experience in performing what appear to be contradictory functions (277–78).

In their observations on the evolution of prison chaplaincy that underlie the study, Sundt and Cullen's conclusions parallel my own in Chapter Two. Noting that the chaplain's institutional role was originally broad—encompassing such things as education, library operation, and even compilation of statistical reports for legislators—the authors then point to a major shift that took place near the turn of the century.

> With the rise of rationalism and the social sciences, the chaplain became a religious representative in a secularized institution of professionals. Furthermore, when the role of religion in the prison was marginalized, the chaplaincy was diminished with it. The duties that the chaplain had traditionally performed were largely taken over by professionals and specialists. (273)

From that point, the chaplain's role became increasingly ambiguous and both their relevance and value were called into question.

> Rather than recede to the periphery, however, chaplains have traditionally attempted to recast the nature of their work. The history of the chaplaincy from 1900 to the present, therefore, has been characterized by efforts to maintain legitimacy and to negotiate a position of value outside of a strictly spiritual role . . . the chaplaincy's value began to be tied to its ability to serve institutional needs. (273–74)

Sundt and Cullen then trace a series of redefinitions by chaplains. In the Progressive Era, they saw their primary role as educator-reformers (soul doctors and moral physicians); during the 1930s and 1960s, influenced by the rehabilitative ideal, chaplains worked to become part of the treatment teams and added training in psychology and CPE to their credentials; the 1970s brought the era of ecumenism to the profession, and chaplains became advocates for inmate's newly established religious freedoms; eventually, they have tied their value to their ability to facilitate inmate management (274).

These factors are partly to blame for both the ambiguity of their roles and the conflict that produces. But other things exacerbate the problem, as the researchers point out. For one thing, chaplains occupy a middle ground between inmate and prison staff and must constantly balance their responsibilities and obligations to both. For another, chaplains also have affiliations outside the prison with their church and/or denomination, and these entities also have a set of expectations of the chaplains that may be inconsistent with those of the secular institution (278–79). Truly, the chaplain occupies terrain that is difficult to successfully navigate. In spite of these things, however, this study did not produce evidence of any significant role ambiguity, though role conflicts appeared to vary considerably among the chaplain-respondents (290–93).

More pertinent to our present considerations, though, are Sundt and Cullen's exploration of chaplaincy tasks. Utilizing descriptions from five brief articles, as well as Shaw's text (see above) and a G.L. Murphy's 1956 doctoral dissertation on the "social role" of the chaplain, the researchers compiled a list of 24 most frequently mentioned activities. The chaplains were then asked to assess the amount of time they devoted to each activity on a scale of 1–10, with 1 equaling "no time" and 10 equal to "almost all of the time" (281–82). In some cases, the task list is quite precise; for instance the list includes "helping inmates make plans for their release", "helping inmates adjust to prison," and even "encouraging inmates to repent." In other instances, the task list is remarkably broad: There are items designated "paperwork," "religious education," and "coordinating religious programs." These sorts of distinction may be partly a product of the researcher's dependence on a small list of selected research articles, which of course reflects both the limited attention paid to the chaplaincy by students of penology and the failure of chaplains, themselves, to create an adequate literature of their profession. The flaws in the task list may also stem from a limited knowledge or misperceptions the researchers have concerning the various chaplaincy functions, as we shall discuss below.

Sundt and Cullen grouped these tasks into five categories and ranked them on the basis of their mean scores according to the amount of time spent on each. (Within each of the top three categories, though, there were individual tasks that ranked in the top ten most time-consuming activities.) Here is the list, in descending order:

1. Administrative/organizational tasks
2. Services to inmates
3. Religious activities
4. Assistance to other correctional staff
5. Community relations

Although this is a useful approach to an understanding of chaplaincy roles, the items divided between the second and third categories may demonstrate a misunderstanding by the authors of the pastoral function of chaplaincy. The following tasks were among those considered to be *services to inmates*:

- Counseling
- Helping inmates adjust to prison
- Visiting inmates in isolation or segregation
- Counseling and helping inmate families
- Visiting sick inmates
- Counseling inmates on death row

From the perspective of a chaplain, each of these duties takes place within a pastoral context, but Sundt and Cullen do not identify these as *religious activities*. Another of the items in category 2—"helping inmates make plans for their release"—would surely involve faith-based strategies; a chaplain's approach to this issue is quite distinct from that of the inmate's caseworker. Four of the items listed in the *services to inmates* category ranked in the top ten of time expenditure, and only a single item in the category is clearly devoid of a pastoral element: "teaching general education."

Sundt and Cullen wrestled with this as they assessed the relationships between the sacred and secular. They conclude that chaplains "spend most of their time performing secular duties," but the researchers reject the notion that activities related to counseling are sacred, though they offer no evidence to support their assertions.

. . . the four most frequently performed tasks—counseling, coordinating religious programs, paperwork, and supervising volunteers—are of a secular nature. Furthermore, conducting religious services and teaching religious education are the only strictly spiritual tasks ranked among the ten most frequently performed duties. Likewise, when chaplains' tasks are categorized, we find that on the average, chaplains spend more time on administrative and/or organizational tasks and providing inmates with services then they spend on religious activities . . . when chaplains were asked to rank the importance of five primary tasks, chaplains typically assigned the greatest importance to counseling inmates. Although chaplains may approach counseling from a spiritual standpoint, the task of counseling is arguably a secular duty. (287)

Most chaplains, I am convinced, would argue exactly the opposite—counseling inmates is clearly a pastoral duty. The researchers recognize that to be the case and speak to the point, yet they reject the chaplain's viewpoint out of hand! More than that, religious counseling is at the very core of the chaplain's pastoral role within the facility and is the primary mark of distinction between them and any other social services staff member.

> *Researchers continue to have difficulty delineating just what the chaplain does and how those tasks interface with penological or custodial goals. That ambiguity is related to the growing marginalization of religion in correctional institutions, which has been at least partly engendered by the chaplain's willingness to reinvent themselves.*

These conclusions illustrate the fact that these researchers, like others before them, continue to have difficulty delineating just what the chaplain does and how those tasks interface with penological or custodial goals. That ambiguity is related to the growing marginalization of religion in correctional institutions, which has been at least partly engendered by the chaplain's willingness to reinvent themselves. These concerns are at the center of a later study by Sundt and Cullen: *"Doing God's Work Behind Bars: Chaplains' Reactions to Employment in Prison"* (2007). Here, they utilized the same data from their 1998 research to further examine the occupational experiences of prison chaplains from two perspectives: the absolute levels of both job satisfaction and work stress; and the degree to which time spent on administrative tasks, rather than direct ministry, contributed to job stress or influenced their satisfaction with their work (140).

For chaplains, as is true for other prison employees, work experiences are shaped by job characteristics. "In particular role conflict was the strongest predictor of both job satisfaction and work stress . . . Job dangerousness was also found to affect prison chaplains' levels of work stress" (149). On the other hand, "Age, gender, race, education, and religious denomination were unrelated to chaplains' reactions to working in prison" (150). Nonetheless, the researchers found that chaplains were very positive about their work.

> Despite persistent cultural and legal doubts about the appropriate role of religion in American prisons and shifting occupational expectations, prison chaplains are remarkably happy employees who appear to cope well with the demands of their work. This study found that virtually all of the chaplains studied were very satisfied or somewhat satisfied with their jobs. A general comparison of these results to those found in other studies of correctional employees suggests that prison chaplains feel more positively about their work than their colleagues . . . they report low to moderate levels of work stress. (149)

A close analysis of these data provides additional insights that are important to our current considerations. The authors concluded that "Time spent on administrative tasks and coordinating religious programs was associated with greater levels of work stress. We also observed a positive, though weak, relationship between performing religious tasks and job satisfaction" (150). Considering the fact that in the initial data distribution, counseling was identified as a secular task, it is easy to extrapolate that if those data were reclassified as religious, the designated "weak relationship" would appear to be much stronger. Then there is this tantalizing observation:

> The results point to a potential drawback of shifting to a model of prison chaplaincy that emphasizes administration and co-ordination of religious programs. The more effort devoted to administrative activities, the more stressed chaplains will likely become. It seems probable too that an increased emphasis on administration and coordination of religious programs will contribute to role problems. (150)

These conclusions are remarkable, coming as they do from academicians rather than chaplains. They also appear to contradict the ease with which some prominent chaplaincy spokespersons have advocated for a primary role as quasi-legal counsel for constitutional religious matters, as we noted in the previous chapter.

A thorough review of the entire body of correctional literature reveals curious contradictions. While many items attest to the important role of religion in the history and practices of penology as well as in the lives of offenders, few substantive works address the chaplaincy itself. Much of what does exist is either anecdotal or polemical and doesn't contribute to a scholarly exploration of the profession or provide any useful schematic of the overall role functions of correctional chaplaincy. Those that do carefully and objectively treat the subject often focus on a specific function, e.g., counseling, working with staff, etc., rather than considering the full range of duties associated with the job. The works reviewed here offer substantial insights into the broad dimensions of correctional chaplaincy. The remainder of this text will expand on these ideas by presenting a paradigm for chaplaincy that incorporates the wide range of chaplaincy tasks into a unified ministry model that takes into account the often contradictory expectations inherent with the position. In addition, it will provide an analytic tool useful for creating a strategic plan of delivering chaplaincy services in any institution.

REFERENCES

Covert, Henry G. (1995). *Ministry to the Incarcerated*. Chicago: Loyola University Press.

Pace, Dale K. (1976). *A Christian's Guide to Effective Jail & Prison Ministries*. Old Tappen, NJ: Fleming H. Revel.

Shaw, Richard Denis. (1995). *Chaplains to the Imprisoned: Sharing Life with the Incarcerated*. New York: The Haworth Press.

Sundt, Jody L. & Francis T. Cullen. (1998). The Role of the Contemporary Prison Chaplain. *The Prison Journal* 78 (3): 271–98.

Sundt, Jody L. & Francis T. Cullen. (2008). Doing God's Work Behind Bars: Chaplains' Reactions to Employment in Prison. *Journal of Offender Rehabilitation*, 45 (3): 131–57.

Chapter Four

A Paradigm for Chaplaincy: The Critical Dimensions

There is the story about a verbal exchange that took place between a baseball catcher and the home plate umpire. A pitch arrived at the plate in an area that the catcher was confident would be called a strike, but instead he heard the umpire call out, "Ball."

The catcher immediately challenged the ump. "No way was that a ball! It was right over the heart of the plate. That's got to be a strike in anybody's league."

To which the umpire replied: "A pitch ain't nothing until I call it something, and then whatever I call it, that's what it is!"

The story is relevant to correctional chaplaincy. The notion of what exactly a chaplain is and what tasks should be central to role performance have fluctuated over time, as we have noted. In order to survive in the rapidly shifting correctional environment, chaplains have perhaps too easily embraced a model for their professional position that is being shaped and defined by other correctional stakeholders. In the process they may have given away their pastoral birthright. To whatever degree chaplains surrender the territory of the transcendent and the specific religious functions of

49

their call to become penological strategists who perform primarily secular tasks, their office as "keeper of the cloak" is proportionally diminished.

Being asked to function as both a government employee and a representative of a transcendent God creates certain conflicts. Ideally, the jail or prison chaplain represents and symbolizes the presence of a higher implied authority. But under whose authority does the chaplain function? More importantly, if a tension develops between the orders of the state and the commands of God, how does the chaplain respond? He or she must forge some sort of an alliance between the earthly and the heavenly in an effort to meet the requirements of the office of chaplaincy. It is an uneasy alliance, one that is in constant tension, but successful institutional chaplains develop creative strategies to meet the demands of both authorities. Theoretically at least, the relationship between church and government is negotiable. Once again, the comments of Canadian Chaplain J.T.L. James are salient.

> No one can seriously challenge the fact that the chaplains' ultimate authority is God, and their primary loyalty must be to the religious authorities who, through ordination or other accreditation, give them their mandate to exercise the special ministry of chaplaincy. It is because they hold that ecclesiastical status that they are engaged by the secular authority to serve as chaplains in its institutions; should they, for any reason, lose that mandate they would no longer be qualified for the position.

> Governments exercise their right to set standards for chaplaincy and select the persons who meet their criteria, but they cannot create chaplains; chaplaincy is a ministry of the church or other faith group which only those it mandates can deliver. The employing authority, fulfilling its responsibility for the spiritual well-being of its inmates, engages chaplains to carry out the ministry which the churches define. (James 111)

From a practical standpoint, however, the chaplain is in place to carry out an institutional program developed around goals that match systemic concerns rather than to promote a church-initiated enterprise with purely theological aims. Every chaplain must deal with a divided allegiance: He or she must be a supervisor of programs for the system, yet at the same time be a pastor to inmates, empathizing with their plight and serving their needs. In some cases, the role of chaplain conflicts with that of institutional supervisor; it is not unusual for the chaplain to become a quasi-negotiator between staff and inmates who have developed instinctive adversarial relationships.

Religion may serve two purposes in a correctional institution. First, it fulfills constitutional rights established by government. By itself, this is sufficient grounds for having *the presence of religious opportunities*, but it does not necessarily dictate either the necessity for religious programs or the utilization of chaplains. Second, religion provides *inherent value* to the institution, apart from any legal mandates. If the latter is true, then both chaplains and religious programs are important. The first purpose might be met with any administrative personnel and/or processes; the latter argues for an informed deliverer of religious services. In a real sense, then, the value of chaplains rests on any *accrued institutional* value religion can demonstrate—if it has value, so does the chaplain.

> *In a correctional arena that reflects our culture's ambivalence towards the notion of an omnipotent God, and in a venue where resources are severely stretched, it is essential that religious programs satisfy secular goals if they are to survive.*

But for religion to have value to the institution, it must fulfill secular goals, not just religious ones. It has not always been that way; in the past American culture accepted a foundational *a priori* assumption of faith in a Supreme Being. Now, however, religion is no longer privileged. Instead, it must take its place alongside numerous secular pursuits as one item on a menu of optional life choices. Similarly, in correctional programming, religious services are merely one of several institutional endeavors that must demonstrate worthiness in order to continue to be listed on a highly competitive menu of options. In a correctional arena that reflects our culture's ambivalence towards the notion of an omnipotent God, and in a venue where resources are severely stretched, it is essential that religious programs satisfy secular goals if they are to survive. This has been problematic, as we shall see.

From a penological perspective, religious goals only have meaning to correctional systems if it can be shown that they concurrently satisfy institutional goals. For instance, a primary (religious) goal of Christianity is to be faithful to Christ and to glorify God through one's life. In the process of that faithful walk, radical changes may take place in the lives of believers, one of which could be a commitment to law-abiding behavior. This new behavior, then, would be a by-product of Christian conversion. However, rehabilitation is a primary (secular) goal of correctional agencies and, from the agency's perspective, it does not matter whether the behavioral change is a result of religious conversion or any other motivating factor. Conversion is a spiritual issue, while rehabilitation is primarily an ethical and moral one (see Pace 1985). So, institutional goals related to the changing of lives—rehabilitation—are not identical with the goals of the chaplaincy. Religion can be a tool of rehabilitation for prison administrators, but from a pastoral perspective, it is something that, though related, is also quite different.

Like others on the prison treatment team, one of the chaplain's significant roles is to help inmates face the truth about themselves and help them find the strength to change. Unlike other professional care givers, however, the successful chaplain understands that lasting life change best takes place within the context of faith in a living, empowering God. Brockway and other idealists at the 1870 Prison Congress envisioned the reformation of offenders; but to reform is to "improve by correction or removal of defects." The chaplain, on the other hand, is interested in regeneration, which entails the spiritual and moral reformation of the individual and takes place only in concert with the Divine. Indeed, the process of internalized attitudinal and behavioral change might easily be expressed in religious terms as repentance and conversion—a change in life direction controlled by a renewed center of being. Thus, chaplains walk a difficult path between the sacred and secular dominions.

Until recently, very little research existed that could speak to the issue of how religion impacted dysfunctional behavior. Indeed, as long as the culture accepted God and the worthiness of His goals, what need was there of proof that God's goals had any additional value? We accepted the tautology: since God is good, His goals are also good. But a growing correctional professionalism brought with it an increased demand for empirical evidence of program value and eventually eroded that sacred platform. When asked to verify that religion worked, chaplains could offer only anecdotal support which, though having some validity, could not overcome the demands to demonstrate results based on more rigorous research principles. As late as 1984, Byron Johnson could summarize, "The question of whether rehabilitation and treatment of offenders is enhanced by religious training is an empirical question which has not yet been examined" (Johnson 1984:13). Fortunately, we now have some sound research that documents the work of correctional ministries.

> *In recent years, several well-designed empirical studies have demonstrated the positive relationship between religious commitment and both lowered recidivism and positive institutional behavior.*

At its core, to demonstrate the usefulness of religious programs to correctional officials, one must show that they in fact work; in other words, that they meet institutional goals. While some religious practitioners would prefer to confine their activities to the sacred realm and are uncomfortable with those who insist on measuring their impact in terms of secular behaviors, today's correctional environment demands precisely that. The truth is that standardized outcomes for religious practices can never measure the full work of chaplaincy. On the other hand, just because some part of what chaplains deliver cannot be measured, that is not to say that significant portions can't be.

Most recent research has focused on two measures of effectiveness. First, *does involvement with religious programs rehabilitate?* From a research perspective, rehabilitation is most often equated to lower recidivism rates, since these can be quantifiably measured. Second, *does religious involvement alter institutional behavior?* The first concern is more directly related to the philosophical goals of those agencies that oversee individual institutions—departments of corrections or county or regional jail administrations—as well as to the public that supports and funds those agencies. The second measure more directly impacts day-to-day operations of the correctional facility, and for those who work behind the walls, is arguably more important.

> *Chaplains must stake out and defend an institutional territory that is essentially a "no man's land," personifying love and compassion in the process, and confronting issues that are relegated to their province alone.*

In recent years, several well-designed empirical studies have demonstrated the positive relationship between religious commitment and both lowered recidivism and positive institutional behavior. Byron R. Johnson summarizes these and other studies that measure the impact of religion on crime in his *More God, Less Crime* (2011). His text is exhaustive, and I will not attempt a thorough review of the portions that deal specifically with prison populations; however, some observations may be extracted from these studies that are quite relevant to our discussion. First, religious programs have inherent value to correctional institutions because they meet institutional goals. Second, religious programs are not a panacea. It will not solve all inmate adjustment problems, nor help to rehabilitate every prisoner, but what we know is that religion works for some inmates, under some conditions, some of the time. Can more than that be said about any other prison program directed at inmate adjustment or rehabilitation? (See, too, Johnson 2012.)

Clearly, the degree to which religious programming may impact inmate behavior is highly dependent on the ability of chaplains to properly discern the characteristics of both their environment and their participants, and to appropriately adjust and effectively deliver their program services accordingly. This was emphasized by one of the most comprehensive studies of the impact of religion on inmate adjustment:

> The key factors that molded a particular religious program were
> the characteristic of the prison, the chaplain, and the inmate so-

cial system. We concluded that an interactive relationship exists between the inmate, the prison, the religious programming, and the type and degree of institutional adjustment. (Clear et al 24)

Chaplains must stake out and defend an institutional territory that is essentially a "no man's land," personifying love and compassion in the process, and confronting issues that are relegated to their province alone. For instance, what does delivering "good news" in a jail or prison setting look like? How does one challenge inmates to commit to the principles of a faith in a dehumanizing place where the physical realities of existence may never get better? Can we bring a liberating message into the institution, free from contradictions, distortions, and confusion?

As former Texas chief of chaplains Emmett Solomon has stated, "Systems cannot love; people love. Systems can serve, but they do so without love. They are efficient, but impersonal, and they don't make us feel good." Solomon identifies four essentials employed in raising children to be responsible adults that are also necessities for correcting human behavior: 1) love, 2) guidance, 3) nourishment or nurture, and 4) discipline. "Jails and prisons," says Solomon, "can only offer guidance and discipline; they are incapable of providing either love or nurture" (Solomon). This is the domain of the correctional chaplain, and it can be filled by no other member of the institutional team.

While prison systems don't claim love and nurture as part of their goals, religious faiths do. However, a conflict may again arise because mission statements of correctional chaplaincy services are usually expressed in terms of legal objectives rather than religious goals. If we were to examine the mission statement of the chaplaincy component of almost any correctional agency, we would find some language about facilitating opportunities for inmates to pursue their individual religious beliefs and practices within the guidelines of established policy. The focus of the mission centers on the opportunity to practice one's personal beliefs rather than the outcome of that practice. This may seem a trivial distinction, but it clearly expresses what we have already identified as the main concern of prison officials in the past decade—upholding individual rights to practice any recognized religion. The mission statement would probably also include a reference to assisting inmates to become productive citizens—rehabilitation—but with a caveat that this takes place only if the inmate chooses a religious pathway to that goal. Here, too, the distinctive is centered on a constitutional right.

The *Establishment Clause* of the First Amendment prohibits the State from establishing any religion. In the current political and legal environment, pluralistic philosophies dictate that Christianity is only one item on a menu of available religious choices. In addition, the *Establishment Clause* must be balanced against the *Free Practice Clause* of the Constitution, which forbids the state to prohibit inmates from practicing their religion unless that practice conflicts with the secure and orderly operation of the institution. Passage of federal laws such as the Religious Land Use and Institutionalized Persons Act (RLUIPA) has mandated that institutions cannot impose any substantial burden on the religious exercise of incarcerated individuals and that any restrictions made must: 1) be in the furtherance of a compelling governmental interest, and 2) be the "least restrictive" means of restraint of those practices. Increasingly, systemic concern with individual rights has significantly altered the role of the correctional chaplain.

Indeed, most prison systems now primarily regard chaplains as program managers, quite at odds with the 1774 Act of the British Parliament inspired by John Howard. This act provided for chaplains, outlining certain specific duties. ". . . he shall read morning and evening prayers each Sunday, Good Friday, and Christmas. . . preach two sermons each Sunday. . . all offenders shall attend." The chaplain was to visit ". . . any of the offenders, either sick or in health, that may desire or stand in the need of his spiritual advice and attendance" (James 62–63). This short list of services rendered, however, bears only scant resemblance to the duties a modern institutional chaplain must perform.

In an effort to develop a comprehensive task list for contemporary chaplains, over several years I gave all students enrolled in my chaplaincy courses an identical assignment. Based on their limited knowledge of chaplaincy, each was asked to make a comprehensive list of all the tasks they envisioned a chaplain might be called upon to perform in the course of his or her work routine. They were told to be specific and avoid broad theoretical concepts. Then, as the students interacted with one another, we would compile a composite list—one that soon became quite lengthy. While there may be no such thing as a fully comprehensive list that identifies every possible task, and though staffing structures or management designs vary across institutions, as the spiritual leader of the institution with responsibility for the needs of the entire inmate population, chaplains might have occasion to perform any or all of the following tasks:

- Conduct nondenominational worship services and special celebratory services such as Christmas or Easter.
- Conduct Bible studies.
- Work with various faith group leaders to administrate special activities and diets for inmates (e.g., Ramadan feast; kosher diets).
- Provide access for all faith leaders and schedule activities for their designated groups, e.g., Islamic Imams conducting Jumu'ah Prayer, Jewish Rabbis conducting Sabbath services, or Catholic priests celebrating mass or hearing confessions.
- Coordinate special visits with inmates by outside pastors or faith leaders.
- Schedule all religious programs within the institution—worship services, Bible studies, special events, etc.—and obtain security clearances for those involved.
- Recruit and coordinate volunteers for all religious activities.
- Conduct periodic volunteer training sessions and maintain records of volunteer activities.
- Be present at numerous volunteer-led activities, assisting visitors through security and escorting them to designated areas.
- Develop and lead positive peer support or growth groups.
- Facilitate meeting of special-needs groups, e.g., substance abuse; cognitive skills sessions.
- Conduct intake interviews of newly arrived inmates, informing them of religious opportunities and available resources.
- Counsel with individual inmates about their spiritual growth or personal problems.
- Provide crisis counseling, such as divorce notifications, suicide threats, etc.

- Inform inmates of a death in their family, facilitate phone contacts with other family members and provide grief counseling.
- Coordinate temporary releases and arrange transportation for deathbed visits or attendance at funerals of family members.
- Contact family upon the death of inmate and arrange for body to be released, etc.
- Visit inmates in medical dorms, mental health units, or segregation areas.
- Be present, periodically, on visiting day to interact with families of inmates.
- Liaison with inmate families and social service agencies when special hardships are identified.
- Conduct inmate marriage ceremonies (as permitted).
- Perform baptisms.
- Provide pre-release counseling for inmates preparing for transition to the community.
- Liaison with the outside religious community to assist them in their reentry ministry to inmates or with help for inmate returning to the community.
- Maintain a library of religious books, magazines, and tapes and co-ordinate their circulation.
- Interface with staff and develop relationships to open potential pastoral opportunities.
- Attend or conduct funerals/weddings for staff members.
- Counsel staff members re: their faith journey or with personal life issues.
- Attend staff or special treatment team meetings.
- Serve on designated emergency response teams.
- Manage chaplaincy budget; order equipment and supplies.
- Supervise inmate worker(s) assigned to the chaplaincy area.
- Write periodic reports for facility supervisor and/or supervising chaplain.
- Prepare periodic reports for one's religious denomination or sponsoring agency.
- Represent institution at area churches or community organizations.

- Teach a class at college or seminary and/or supervise internships and practicums.
- Maintain active membership in a local church congregation and participate in denominational activities.
- Pray daily for both the staff and the inmates of the institution.
- Be on-call 24 hours on assigned days.

After creating such a list, I then asked my students to analyze it and to identify large umbrella categories under which each of the tasks might logically fit. For example, there might be several items that could fall under a category they identified as "counseling"; others they might have labeled "teaching", and so forth. This exercise formed the basis for a discussion in which we would further clarify and adjust the categories in an effort to create a working model for institutional chaplaincy, even though we recognized that there was no single correct paradigm. Eventually, I would share my classification system—one that underwent some changes as my students and I learned from each other through the years. Later in the course, students were required to interview a chaplain as the basis for a written field report. At the end of their interview, they shared the categorization of tasks we had developed and asked the chaplains for feedback, which we then added to the mix of our explorations.

In the first of a three-part series of articles written by members of the American Correctional Chaplains Association for publication in Corrections Today, Paul Rogers outlined seven categories of specific duties of correctional chaplains. These also currently appear on the ACCA's website and in a brochure the organization prepared for distribution to jail chaplains.

- Religious program management
- Pastoral counseling
- Primary advisors on religious program policy
- Perform liturgical duties consistent with their own faith groups
- Recruitment, training and coordination of religious volunteers
- Maintain order in the prison through their active presence and influence
- Represent corrections in the outside community (Rogers 77)

(I have only summarized these categories here. The article, itself, provides a more detailed explanation of each.) A quick comparison with the composite list my students and I developed will reveal that most of the items easily fit into one of the seven categories identified by Chaplain Rogers. Some items might not immediately match one of the seven categories, and it would be possible to compress or modify certain of the items for a tighter fit, but none of them violates the essential definitions of Chaplain Rogers' list, and most are highly consistent with them.

I suggest, though, a more succinct grouping—one I developed over time with my students and that resonated well with the many chaplains my students interviewed. Later, when I had the opportunity to supervise a number of chaplains in the field, I found the paradigm served us well. It provides not only a conceptual framework for the position, but also serves as a planning guide for structuring the delivery of chaplaincy services in a way that easily accommodates measurement of program outcomes. The paradigm I offer separates the ministry into three *critical dimensions* that encompass all functions of the chaplaincy.

- Pastoral
- Administrative
- Community

In the chapters that follow, we will unpack each of these three dimensions in more detail. First, however, we need to consider a fourth aspect—one that is foundational to all other dimensions of chaplaincy and from which all ministry flows: the **personal dimension**.

REFERENCES

Clear, T., Stout, B., Dammer, H., Kelly, L., Hardyman, P. & Shapiro, C. (1992). *Prisoners, Prisons and Religion: Final Report*. Newark, New Jersey: School of Criminal Justice, Rutgers University.

James, J.T.L. (1990). *A Living Tradition: Penitentiary Chaplain*. Ottawa: Chaplaincy Division, Correctional Service of Canada.

Johnson, Byron R. (1984). Hellfire and Corrections: A Quantitative Study of Florida Prison Inmates. *Unpublished doctoral dissertation*, Florida State University.

Johnson, Byron R. (2011). *More God, Less Crime*. West Conshohocken, PA: Templeton Press.

Johnson, Byron R. (2012). Can a Faith-Based Prison Reduce Recidivism? *Corrections Today*, 73:60-62.

Pace, D.K. (1985). The Potential of Christianity to Rehabilitate Prisoners. *Journal of the American Scientific Affiliation*, 37(2), 93–95.

Rogers, Paul. (2003) Correctional Chaplains Calming the Storms of Life. *Corrections Today*. (February): 77.

Solomon, Emmett. Address at Coalition of Prison Evangelists conference. Virginia Beach, VA: October 4, 1995.

Chapter Five

Personal Dimension

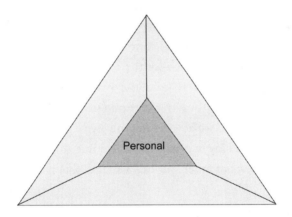

C haplains struggle for professional identity within a system that sends mixed messages about their personal worth and imposes confusing role expectations. This is compounded by their dealings with fellow clergy in the community or even within the chaplain's own denominational structures, nearly all of whom often treat correctional chaplains as less than authentic clergy—as men and women unfit for "real" ministry or unable to survive in the local parish. As a result, chaplains often develop a sense of isolation and futility in their work. Seminaries, intent on producing local pastors, rarely prepare their students to deal with the dynamics of the correctional ministry; thus few chaplains arrive at their initial job with adequate preparation. Most often, they come to their position having sensed a call to serve as pastor and helper only to find themselves primarily accountable for administrative outcomes. Moreover, prisons and jails are filled with a heterogeneous population composed of high-needs individuals, nearly all who have severe problems and few of whom offer supportive undergirding for their minister. This is in stark contrast to the typical free-world congregation, whose members are usually comfortably compatible with one another and who, for the most part, warmly embrace their pastoral staff.

Chaplaincy is also a ministry that provides little in the way of recognition for its practitioners. Failures are the norm. The inmates with whom we work have, in most cases, been experiencing behavioral dysfunctions, making poor decisions, and living in opposition to the law for a substantial portion of their lives; the majority will continue to do so in spite of our efforts to help them grow or change. We are not engaged in a high-percentage ministry. Our call is to seek out the one wandering sheep that has crawled into the crag of a rock; to search for the one lost coin that has rolled into the corner of a dark room; or to point the way to one lost son whose father remains patiently waiting for him to return (*see Luke 15*). But most of our labor will be in vain, and we have to not only live with that, but to somehow find contentment and joy in ministry while doing so. That's a difficult task, and it requires a level of inner spiritual strength that is not easily acquired or maintained.

> *Effective ministry is always directly related to the health of the one performing it, and spiritual health must not only be appropriately formed, it must also be constantly nourished.*

Considering this, as well as the other stress factors described by Sundt and Cullen or Shaw (Chapter Three) that are endemic to the demanding and diverse responsibilities required of the fully orbed position (Chapter Four), it becomes immediately evident that chaplains must be healthy in every aspect of their being—physical, mental, and spiritual. Otherwise, they will not survive in their profession very long, let alone be effective in this exacting ministry. It is crucial, then, that chaplains pay close attention to their personal growth and spiritual health. What that looks like will differ rather dramatically from person to person and is not easily framed in any generic context. Still, the point this chapter emphasizes is foundational: *Effective ministry is always directly related to the health of the one performing it, and spiritual health must not only be appropriately formed, it must also be constantly nourished.* As Will Rogers reminded us, "Even if you're on the right track, you'll get run over if you just sit there."

MAINTAINING A HEALTHY SPIRITUAL RELATIONSHIP

I vividly recall a series of conversations I had over a two- or three-year period with a former director of the Bureau of Prisons Religious Services that illustrates this point. He described the burnout trends among his corps of chaplains, the marriage and family difficulties some of them were experiencing, and the high percentage of chaplains who were disconnected from supportive faith communities due to their heavy engagement with in-facility ministry. In short, their inner spiritual wells had gone dry, and they were struggling to draw enough living water even for themselves, let alone have a sufficient supply to offer to the inmates and staff of their facilities, as well. The director challenged several prison ministry organizations and church congregations to offer a retreat setting for chaplains and their spouses—not for delivery of any continuing education—but simply for the purposes of refreshment and rejuvenation. The dream of that vehicle for renewal went largely unfulfilled, but the problem of spiritually needy chaplains remains with us.

Of course, this problem is not confined to the world of chaplaincy; it is common in other helping professions. For chaplains at least, the problem grows out of a misalignment in our vertical relationship with God. When working with any high-needs clientele, it is all too easy to drift into an attitude of believing that we—not God—are the source of active power. In short, we develop a *Messiah Complex*; though we wouldn't acknowledge it openly, we begin to feel as if we are Jesus to the recipients of our ministry services. Once this notion takes root, we are motivated to try and solve every problem, to do it ourselves, and to work as many hours as it takes to get the job done. Since Jesus has no limits to His power, neither do we.

Since no one else can accomplish what Jesus can, only we are fully capable of fixing the problem being addressed. Since Jesus' spiritual resources are infinite, we, too, need little rest or refueling.

Spiritual health can only thrive when we maintain a proper perspective. We aren't Jesus; we can't fix everything; and there will never be enough hours in the workday to meet every need around us. That conviction isn't a license to work less hard or care less passionately about those to whom we minister—it simply expresses a factual definition of the reality in which we work. We cannot give what we do not have, and if we continue to operate from the Messiah perspective, we will eventually work our way into a dry spiritual well from which we are incapable of delivering any fruitful ministry. Burnout never comes from working too hard; it emerges from an inner dissonance where expectations and demands placed upon us conflict with our accomplishments or abilities. The lack of spiritual health provides a fertile breeding ground for that phenomenon.

So what to do? Get a life! By that I mean that we chaplains must develop and sustain a healthy spiritual life apart from our workplace through worship and fellowship with a body of believers in our communities. A failure to meaningfully participate in activities of a local church not only separates the chaplain from a community supportive of correctional ministry, but it also isolates that chaplain from relationships that sustain his or her personal walk with the Lord. Correctional ministry is draining work. It is carried on within the strongholds of Satan to a group of high-needs individuals whose constant requests for pastoral attention and insatiable appetite for programmed activities can be all-consuming if we allow it to be.

The correctional facility usually has only limited program time available. Moreover, the administration may require that you personally supervise much of the institution's religious activities, creating a situation where the program schedule can easily conflict with the services and activities offered by your own church. To ensure your own spiritual health, you should pay careful attention to scheduling institutional programs in a way that factors your own spiritual activities into the scheduling matrix. Chaplains should not attempt to officiate at every service or religious group activity, and they should share the load with competent and trustworthy volunteers or community ministers. This may mean advocating for adjustment of institutional policies along these lines, but the effort may well determine your professional and spiritual survival. Sacrificing your spiritual needs at the altar of inmate programs is not an acceptable option. God neither expects nor accepts your spiritual martyrdom on behalf of ministry objectives.

Of course, spiritual well-being does not grow in a vacuum; it is nurtured within physical, mental, and social contexts. So chaplains should also cultivate other activities that contribute to personal health in these areas so that they function as a unified instrument of God's grace and mercy. As one of my mentors once commented, "Chaplains walk a tightrope within the institution, trying to faithfully serve both the administration and the inmate population, and you can't walk a tightrope if you're out of balance!"

MAINTAINING EFFECTIVE PERSONAL RELATIONSHIPS

While I can point to no study that specifically investigates the interpersonal and familial relationships of chaplains, I can attest to anecdotal evidence that this is an area of concern for those who supervise them. With no data with which to compare professional pastors in other arenas, we can only discuss points of divergence with a theoretical ideal. Scripture presents clear models for desirable family units and interpersonal relationships, as well as for interactions within the brotherhood of faith and with other societal structures. Nearly every inmate with which the chaplain works has had serious problems appropriately navigating those territorial waters, so it is critical that the chaplain be able to offer constructive options for them to consider as a means of overcoming their past deficiencies. Can the chaplain do that with any authenticity if he or she is either seriously failing in this area of their own life or unable to legitimately model the things being taught?

> *We must learn to be receivers as well as givers, and allow ourselves to be ministered to even as we offer ministry to others. This process happens most effectively within close interpersonal relationships. If we fail to properly cultivate these healthy connective linkages, we place ourselves at risk.*

Here, too, perspective is crucial. Ministry must flow out of one's personal life journey. No one can expect to do more than go through the motions and survive day-to-day if our personal relationships are deficient. For those with spouses and/or children, this means setting aside designated times for family activities and treating special occasions in the lives of friends and loved ones as essential and nonnegotiable calendar events. These are not merely duties to perform; they are life-giving sustenance to the chaplain's own health and well-being as they both lovingly give and graciously receive God's blessings from others. Too often, we set ourselves atop a peak from which we reach down to those in need of our ministry gifts. It is a comfortable perch and is accompanied by the illusion of self-sufficiency, if not invincibility. But we must learn to be receivers as well as givers, and allow ourselves to be ministered to even as we offer ministry to others. This process happens most effectively within close interpersonal relationships. If we fail to properly cultivate these healthy connective linkages, we place ourselves at risk.

SUSTAINING AN ACTIVE AGENDA FOR PROFESSIONAL DEVELOPMENT

Given the difficulties chaplains consistently face in their work environment, professional development is essential—not optional. Yet, even as we accept this axiom, we find the pathway to achievement unpaved and strewn with barriers. For one thing, there are few continuing education opportunities. As discussed earlier, courses designed specifically for training potential or emerging chaplains are almost nonexistent. The same is true for any continuing education offerings designed specifically to enhance correctional ministry.

In addition, there are rarely any institutional funds available for such training even when it can be found. Still, chaplains must solve this dilemma if they intend to enhance their skill set, learn best practices within their arena, or refresh their heart for ministry through exchanges with professional colleagues. With careful planning and the leveraging of outside financial assistance, a workable plan is attainable if there is a sufficient commitment to excellence. Few professions fail to both expect and accommodate an ongoing agenda of professional development, and chaplaincy must find a way to proactively respond to this dearth, something we will address with more specific suggestions in Chapter Ten.

The beginning point for setting any development agenda is a careful, thorough, and honest assessment of one's strengths and weaknesses. There are several useful tools available for this analysis. Those that have been developed in recent years have primarily evolved out of the leadership literature and focus on a strengths-based perspective that advocates building upon one's identified strengths while managing around personal weaknesses. This is not only a legitimate approach for chaplains to adopt, but when paired with an instrument that measures spiritual gifts, it can provide the correctional chaplain with an accurate picture of where he or she can best direct their specific abilities within the wide range of institutional ministry demands.

Once the individual strengths and deficits are identified, each can be addressed accordingly. In the area of strengths, the chaplain should look for any continuing education activities that might sharpen, enhance, or extend that ability. At the same time, the chaplain should thoughtfully assess the tasks required by the position, noting which of those parallel his or her gifts and skills, and which fall within the area of identified weakness. Any mission-critical task that calls for the chaplain to work outside the range of his or her "sweet spot" or within the range of personal deficits is a potential barrier to successful ministry. For these, the chaplain should consider to what degree this deficiency can be overcome through training; by added discipline and attention; or by acceptable modification of the task that will bring it within the range of a personal strength. Often this sort of analysis will highlight places where volunteers, with their differing gifts and skills, can make a major contribution to the chaplaincy program.

Through training, chaplains can improve in their performance in several essential areas: communication and facilitation skills, administrative strategies, awareness and sensitivity to multiple faith groups, and counseling techniques, to name but a few. Certain of these continuing educational resources are available within the correctional systems themselves, and should be utilized by the chaplains who are employed by those systems. Chaplains should also seek out offerings within their church denomination, local academic institutions, community-based nonprofit organizations, or online educational providers. By using available technologies, chaplains can easily graft educational programs into their work schedule and family routines.

Still, there is no assessment tool yet designed that specifically addresses the breadth of psycho-social attributes, vocational skills, and ministry giftings that prepare one for success in this specialized ministry setting. Nor does education alone address certain occupation hazards that accompany the job—things we are unable to control for, that tend to slowly emerge over time, and that can eventually erode the chaplain's heart and mind and cripple ministry effectiveness. For those, the chaplain needs connection with a group of peers, such as is available through regional and national affiliation with the American Correctional Association, or in the case of state appointed chaplains, within their prison system.

Correctional chaplaincy is poorly understood by pastors of local churches, and quite often, by denominational administrators as well. Therefore, the chaplain's ability to build resistance to the pastoral malaise that hovers over the job can best be fortified though associations with others who are experiencing similar frustrations and can offer both supportive fellowship and wise counsel. If funding for regional conferences is unavailable, a chaplain should consider establishing periodic meetings of a more localized group of chaplains or developing a small network of chaplains he or she regularly talks with by phone or Skype. (This approach will be the primary option for county jail or privatized chaplains.) The point is simple: Peer interaction is a significant factor in long term success.

> *As ambassadors of a living God, bringing His transcendent presence into the inner recesses of the jails and prisons of our land, chaplains cannot be content with anything less than a growing competency in every area of their service.*

Most often, we find considerable mismatches between the job demands of institutional chaplaincy and the set of skills and giftings the chaplain most naturally brings to it. The chaplain either: 1) successfully *adapts* and learns how to thrive within the correctional environment; 2) *fails* rather quickly and seeks another ministry venue; or 3) *adjusts* and develops a survival methodology of some sort. The first two of these options are acceptable—they each seek their own level, and things move forward. The third option is more problematic, for within the ranks of the chaplain-survivor there is a broad range of ministry behaviors, many of which are only minimally acceptable and a few of which are wholly inadequate. Too many of these chaplains continue for too long in the profession—maintaining, but performing poorly and without passion. My contention is that these chaplains are also among the most identifiably frustrated and exhibit the greatest degree of role conflict among their peers. They offer little of value to the inmates and staff of their facilities, and they are detrimental to the profession. As ambassadors of a living God, bringing His transcendent presence into the inner recesses of the jails and prisons of our land, chaplains cannot be content with anything less than a growing competency in every area of their service. A robust agenda of professional development is essential to accomplish this.

Chapter Six

Pastoral Dimension

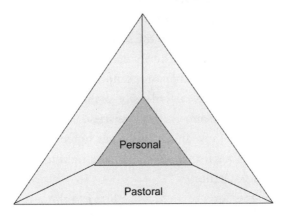

A past colleague who spent many years as the director of his state's Chaplaincy Services Division once told me that there were two critical questions every chaplain should ask him or herself: "By whose authority do you minister within the institution?"; and "What liberation do you bring?" I have always considered that to be excellent advice, for these questions are directed, laser-like, at the core component of the chaplain's identity. In short, they call for an affirmation of the pastoral dimension of chaplaincy, the subject of discussion for this chapter.

Clearly, if chaplains identify the basis of their authority as resting with the State, then the tasks they assume are primarily secular and only secondarily considered as pastoral. While the terms *pastor* or *pastoral* can refer

> *Although Chaplains work within a systemic structure that is established and maintained by a governmental agency and must adhere to the regulations and processes ordained by that entity, their spiritual authority comes from outside that humanly designed structure. The office of pastor cannot be delegated by any governmental agency, and the pastoral dimension of the chaplaincy lies outside its regulatory control.*

to the care and feeding of four-legged wool-bearing animals, when used to describe a professional caregiver within an institutional setting, it always carries a religious and spiritual connotation. So although chaplains work within a systemic structure that is established and maintained by a governmental agency and must adhere to the regulations and processes ordained by that entity, their spiritual authority comes from outside that humanly designed structure. The office of pastor cannot be delegated by any governmental agency, and the pastoral dimension of the chaplaincy lies outside its regulatory control. Chaplains serve a transcendent God for transcendent purposes and must not give up that privilege to temporal authorities. We can only render to Caesar that which he has a right to, and that does not include any spiritual territory.

So, too, the liberation that chaplains bring to those they serve in the institutions cannot be defined or described in purely secular terms. Though chaplains serve the interests of both the state and the citizens of their surrounding communities, their spiritual function lies beyond the parameters of legal definitions. The liberation they bring may yield demonstrable psychological and behavioral changes that parallel penal goals, and as working members of the correctional program team, they commit to and help foster those goals. However, the spiritual freedom that is received by faith, the moral principles that are presented as tenants of that faith, and the lifestyle adjustments that accompany any embracing of it do not emerge from the same reservoir of societal prescriptions. Pastoral authority and the food it offers to those who would partake of it comes only from God and through His Church.

Having said that, we must also acknowledge that at the heart of our pastoral functions is the expectation that those who do choose to embrace God, who accept our counsel, and who become involved in religious activities within the institution will begin to exhibit behavioral change. For most of our history, chaplains have asserted that one of their most valuable institutional roles was that of "agent of change," and until recently most correctional administrators would have agreed. But in an era that emphasizes program facilitation and where the guarantee of the 8th Amendment rights of inmates has become the most sacred duty, that notion has been diminished. This should not be! Genuine faith is far more than a program option or an exercised right. If religious faith has any validity, it should produce measurable change within the individual who embraces it; indeed, this is at the heart of the Gospel message we proclaim.

This is the point where the ministry of chaplaincy intersects with the treatment strategies of other correctional programs. The concept of the tripartite person—physical, mental, spiritual—has traditionally been recognized by Western culture. Institutional program specialists both understand and treat the first two, and they acknowledge the constitutional rights of institutionalized persons to practice the third (even though the chaplain may sometimes question the degree to which these specialist believe it actually exists, or if it does, whether or not it can produce measurable outcomes). Those specialists also recognize that the faith factor is sometimes helpful as a psychological mindset that may contribute to the rehabilitation process.

This is why it is critical for chaplains to maintain a pastoral identity separate and apart from any secular goals of the State. For us, practicing a faith is quite a different thing than acting upon a legal right, and any rehabilitation that takes place is actually a byproduct of our ministry to offenders rather than its primary goal. We function as spiritual caregivers, not as behavioral specialists. Other employees of the institution may counsel or administrate programs and even bear witness to God's activity in the world or their own life, but only the chaplain has the positional authority to speak for and to represent God. He or she is Christ's ambassador—God's designated representative to the prison community. It is an awesome position to hold. As one of my past chaplain associates was fond of proclaiming:

"Being called a chaplain is not something to be proud of; it is a force to be reckoned with!"

SHARING THE GOOD NEWS OF GOD'S LOVE

In many ways, a jail or prison is like the belly of a great whale where men and women have been swallowed by the justice system. The chaplain can be seen as one who sits in the belly, greeting those who arrive with respect as fellow children of God gone seriously astray and offering them comfort, care, and good counsel during their stay. The best solution the criminal system has to offer in response to their behavior is to punish them for their misconduct and separate them from the rest of humanity. It is our privilege, as chaplains, to present them with options for living their lives on different terms. Those whom society and the system see only as problems, we look upon as people of burgeoning potential! Seldom will we have to remind these men and women of their failures, but one of our first challenges will be to help them believe that they are not fully defined by any single act they may have committed, however terrible it might be. We are called to share the incredible news that God not only loves and cares for them in the midst of their failures and destructive behaviors, but that He will share in their present circumstances when they accept His offer of grace.

Given the negative dynamics of institutional life, where hate, fear, bitterness, and loss of self-esteem are the norm, much of the chaplain's efforts are directed toward combating the wide range of interpersonal stress factors that are ever-present in such an environment. Some stressors are predictable, because they are part of an emotional cycle experienced by any incarcerated person. Times of high stress alternate with periods of relative calm as the offender progresses through a series of critical incidents in his or her involvement with the criminal justice system.

When offenders are initially jailed, they usually experience an extremely high level of stress. There is the trauma associated with the arrest: the humiliation of being cuffed and transported to jail; concerns over unfinished business, abandoned personal property, and family members left unattended; potential job loss if the detainee isn't able to bond out; and a generalized uncertainty of what the future holds. Those being incarcerated for the first time are especially traumatized by the sense of loss—loss of freedom, loss of privacy, and loss of security. Eventually, the prisoner adjusts to some degree to the conditions of confinement, and the accompanying stress moderates until the next crisis point is reached and the stress increases once again.

If the inmate doesn't make bond and is forced to remain in jail after the initial hearing, the next stress that begins to build is associated with the approaching trial. Afterwards, if the individual is found guilty, there is an immediate increase to an even higher level of stress which, then begins to abate as the days go on. But then comes the sentence hearing, and stress zooms upward once more, and then again slowly subsides.

Of course, any day may bring some sort of negative news from family members or the deterioration of some personal situation that brings added pressures, and another temporary spike in stress occurs. When sentenced to prison, the inmate gradually becomes more apprehensive with each new day, especially if it is a first prison sentence or if a previous incarceration was a particularly difficult experience. (Inmates disagree on whether or not the fact that they never know which day they will be awakened and put on the bus for the trip to prison makes the waiting easier or more difficult to handle.) These are the personal stressors that all jail inmates endure, and for which the chaplains of those facilities are called upon to helpfully come alongside.

Upon arriving at the prison, the process is repeated. A long series of emotional ups and downs lie ahead; only the specifics of the stress factors have changed. To start with, even as the inmate rides the bus to his or her new prison home, the tension—and often fear—grows in anticipation of what awaits. Those facing their first prison incarceration have heard the stories about how new *fish* are treated; those returning for an additional sentence have already experienced the pressures ahead.

In either case, the first few days of adjustment at the facility are extremely stressful. But for most inmates that eventually levels out, as each discovers a personal pathway for coping with the inherent difficulties of the institutional environment. Still, there are predictable events that will accelerate these emotions to higher levels. Any family-related crisis presents a major stress for the incarcerated person, who can do little to alleviate or respond to any situation outside the walls of the institution. Maybe it is an illness of a child or spouse, or more painful yet, the death of a loved one. Sometimes it is the news that another family member is now in jail. Even the absence of visits or the loss of any communication sends a troubling message to the isolated prisoner. Of course, it is not unusual to receive the *Dear John* or *Dear Jane* letter, or as is sometimes the case, simply a notification from an attorney advising the inmate of a divorce proceeding.

Then there's the parole hearing. When the inmate believes there is a chance for early release, stress will increase exponentially prior to the hearing date and then continue as he or she awaits the decision. Then, if early release is denied, the enormous deflation that follows as the inmate bottoms out creates yet new difficulties. Even when an inmate is granted early release or simply *maxes out*, the pending return to the free world community is—in and of itself—stressful. The inmate knows something about the adjustment difficulties that lie ahead and a great deal about the way he or she handled freedom and behavioral choices in the past, so reentry to society can be an intimidating process to anticipate. Throughout this roller-coaster journey of emotions, the prison chaplain is readily available to listen, to offer direction, to make referrals to helpful resources, and most of all to embody the unconditional love of Christ.

This list of stressors doesn't identify a host of other potential interpersonal conflicts with staff or other inmates in an environment where anger, frustration, and tension are the norm, and where hopelessness is axiomatic. Nor does it speak to any of the intrapersonal deficits that most inmates carry with them wherever they go and that present themselves—often unpredictably—with some frequency. These alone are the source of a great number of problems to which the correctional chaplain may have cause to address. This recurring pattern of rapid increases in level of stress, followed by either a sharp emotional falloff or a more leisurely, but constant, decrease in anxiety has led me to advocate what I refer to as the **Spike and Dip** approach to the pastoral dimension of chaplaincy. Chaplains should consider these predictable stress-inducing events and the aftermath that accompanies them as opportunities to touch the life of an inmate for Christ or to reinforce God's presence in the inmate's life. When anxiety is high, frustration at its peak or depression all-consuming, the potential for acceptance of a new lifestyle or the need for a reminder of God's concern for His children is optimal. Therefore, an effective chaplain will allocate time and establish programs to engage the prisoner during these critical occasions. In Chapter Nine, we will see how this strategy factors into the design of a strategic institutional ministry plan. For now, it is enough to point to these occasions as the primary focal point for most activity surrounding the pastoral dimension we are discussing here.

OFFERING SUPPORTIVE COUNSELING

Within the pastoral component, the ministry of counseling makes the greatest demands on the chaplain's energy and time. This is true for two reasons. First, the stress factors discussed, inherent to prison life, are dynamic rather than static stressors. Emerging from the contexts of daily routines and activities in the corrosive prison environment, they continually evolve and thus demand ongoing attention from the chaplain. Created by the deprivation of one's freedom and aggravated by the dehumanizing prison environment, they are punctuated with a strong sense of loss—of personal identity; of any real autonomy; of the rights to personal privacy; and of unregulated contact with their family and friends. In short, incarceration is a direct assault on the individual psyche.*

Furthermore, the problems that arise as a result always seem to need immediate attention; they are permeated with a sense of urgency. In a world that affords prisoners little control over any but their most basic functions, they often try desperately to control something—for instance, the response of a chaplain to a perceived crisis. Manipulation may be their only readily available source of power. Much of the chaplain's effectiveness is directly proportional to the ability to distinguish authentic needs from perceived ones and to appropriately prioritize the many requests for his or her services.

Second, any long-established intrapersonal deficits that generate the destructive behaviors of those individuals who typically make up the correctional population are seldom altered merely because they hear God's love proclaimed and make some sort of verbal declaration of belief. Authentic change cannot be coerced or manipulated; it emerges slowly, growing out of a unified chaplaincy program with a multifaceted approach to the demographics and specific needs of the inmate population. Any initial responses by the inmate to the communicated love of God must be followed by the more difficult, lengthier process of identifying the sources of individual behavioral problems and developing strategies to address them that can lead to meaningful changes in character and lifestyle. Dealing with the difficult psychological and behavioral issues that are expressed through the lives of offenders is a complex task for the prison chaplain, and it requires effective counseling skills.

When counseling inmates with serious psychological anomalies, chaplains soon discover that offering prayer and scriptural insight in and of itself is seldom effective in eliciting behavioral change. Unfortunately, the chaplain's seminary or bible college education probably included course work only in pastoral counseling and (perhaps) introductory psychology, neither of which provides a sufficient background for therapeutic intervention with these inmates.

Conversely, the secular counselor works under the opposite handicap; he or she attempts to evoke meaningful change in the absence of any scripturally based moral framework. Both approaches produce a high degree of failure. A merger of the two methodologies seems the obvious answer to this dilemma, but such a strategy is easier to describe than to enact. Some chaplains take additional course work in the social sciences to better prepare themselves for this portion of their ministry. Others rely on their CPE training to provide necessary insights for the counseling dimension of their work. In either case, they usually try to position themselves within the institution as legitimate members of the treatment team that also includes the secular counseling component of the facility. This positioning is fraught with difficulty, and many times chaplains are unable to maintain their authentic pastoral identity in this configuration. Either the chaplain tends to become a clinician, abandoning the unique role of spiritual leader, or he or she is neutralized by those treatment team members who deny the spiritual dimension of the human personality or who see it, at best, as only a sometimes-useful appendage to the psychological help they offer.

This is not to say chaplains shouldn't attempt to merge valid scientific insights and effective methodology from the social science disciplines, for God is the author of all truth, whether it is transmitted by the theologian or the psychologist. But chaplains may find they best apply their unified approaches within the framework of designated pastoral programs. This arrangement has the added benefit of clearly distinguishing the chaplain from other administrative personnel, a distinction that often helps make the chaplain more acceptable to the inmate population, too.

The most effective chaplains use an eclectic approach to their counseling opportunities—they draw from a variety of theories and develop a unique personal style. In certain Christian arenas, however, this process sometimes meets with resistance for one of two reasons. First, there are those practitioners who would insist that the particular characteristics they cherish are sacred and must be considered fundamental components of any Christian counseling strategy. Second, a small but rather vocal minority of church leaders have a strong bias against any secular counseling principles. In point of fact, both of these viewpoints spring from a common root: the notion that Scripture is the only appropriate mediator of lifestyle change, a matter already discussed here. Wise chaplains acknowledge that just as there are many Christian therapists who offer biblically sound counseling paradigms, there are also a number of secular theorists and practitioners who provide helpful counseling tools that address various behavioral issues that are commonly associated with offenders. Chaplains should draw on both.

Counseling in the institutional setting primarily takes place in one of three modes. First, a chaplain may interact one-on-one with an inmate in a **formal setting**, usually the chaplain's office. This contact is normally initiated by the prisoner who requests to see the chaplain about a specific problem, though an appointment might be suggested by the chaplain in response to some discussion with the inmate. On the other hand, **informal one-on-one counseling** can take place anywhere within the correctional facility and may grow out of the demands of some immediate circumstance or spring forth naturally out of a spontaneous conversation. (Some may not even consider this type encounter to be a legitimate counseling activity, occurring as it so often does within the context of normal daily routine. But if the chaplain provides any "counsel"—however informal the conversation or unplanned the meeting—it qualifies as a counseling engagement.) Finally, the chaplain may conduct **structured group counseling** sessions. These may center on some shared programmatic characteristic of the group that the chaplain has been assigned to direct—substance abuse or anger management, for example. Or, more infrequently, these may be growth groups—small cell groups that meet regularly to discuss common concerns and offer mutual support—that the chaplain has initiated.

The decision to use a particular counseling mode depends partially on the situation which arises and partially on the chaplain's assessment of his or her individual gifts and abilities. For instance, informal one-on-one counseling will inevitably occur, although how much depends largely on the amount of time chaplains spend outside their immediate program area. Chaplains who make a point of systematically visiting diverse areas of the institution and initiating conversations with inmates in work or recreational areas will discover many informal counseling opportunities. On the other hand, unless conducting groups is specifically mandated as part of treatment, the organization of such groups will probably occur only if the chaplain has identifiable skill sets that match a program need and if that chaplain feels comfortable and competent in facilitating groups.

> *Trusting relationships, not academically astute techniques, provide the beginning point for successful interventions. Trust never originates outside the context of relationships, and relationships take time to develop.*

In the jail setting, a lack of available space and/or necessary restrictions on inmate movement will reduce or even eliminate the group scenario, and may also determine where either of the other options can take place. The formal one-on-one mode will always provide the major portion of chaplaincy counseling interactions, since it is determined by situational need factors rather than selective processes. The fact that this type of contact is inmate-driven also prevents any perception of proselytizing, something every chaplain has to be careful to avoid. In any event, there is never a shortage of inmates who have problems they wish to discuss or requests they hope the chaplain can fulfill.

Regardless of the specifics of the counseling approach or the particular ways it is implemented, one axiom clearly emerges: Trusting relationships, not academically astute techniques, provide the beginning point for successful interventions. Trust never originates outside the context of relationships, and relationships take time to develop. Thus it is the ability of the chaplain to establish and maintain such relationships that is the primary determinant of success. Carl Rogers, developer of *person-centered therapy*, identifies three conditions that are necessary for successful intervention: The counselor must 1) establish empathy with the person he or she is attempting to help; 2) exhibit unconditional personal regard for that person; and 3) demonstrate genuineness (Meador and Rogers 143). Each of these is consistent with Scriptural principles, and should form the basis of any pastoral counseling efforts. Respect, regard, and acceptance must be offered without charge to maximize any pastoral impact.

LEADING WORSHIP, PROVIDING RELIGIOUS INSTRUCTION, AND PROMOTING SPIRITUAL GROWTH

Though counseling may take up the greatest amount of a chaplain's time, it is the delivery of God's Word that most clearly defines the chaplain's role in the institution. A significant part of in-facility counseling can be and is done by other staff members, and in a growing number of institutions, the management of religious programs has even been delegated to non-clergy staff, even though that strategy has serious deficits (as discussed elsewhere in this book). However, in the preaching, teaching, and facilitating of worship—the proclaiming of God's Word—it is only the chaplain who can speak with the authority that accompanies his or her appointment to an ambassadorship (see *2 Cor. 5:18–20*). It is the responsibility and the great joy of the chaplain to coordinate an integrated program of worship and study opportunities that directs the inmate's walk with the Lord— from spiritual birth to spiritual maturity.

A review of the chaplain's task list provided in Chapter Four will uncover a rather small number of items focusing on worship or Christian education. Yet, if we were to look at the schedule of religious activities for most prisons and jails of any size, we would discover some programs taking place nearly every night of the week. Moreover, such is the abundance of worship services or Bible studies that the chaplain often has to turn away volunteer groups who want to provide additional services. Of course, the chaplain doesn't lead all of these efforts, a fact we will discuss at some length in a later chapter, but the chaplain must coordinate these efforts to ensure they meet the needs of the inmate population.

Several points should be considered when designing a chaplaincy program to meet the total needs of the prison population. The physical potentials or limitations of the particular facility may well determine the extent and perhaps even the nature of the program offerings. Similarly, the institutional program design may be tailored to specific inmate population or connected with community resources in a way that impacts chaplaincy program delivery as well. Finally, the demographics of each prison should in some degree determine not only the variety of services, but also the very nature of the worship and educational programs. We will discuss these, along with other factors to consider in the development of an individualized chaplaincy program plan in great detail in Chapter Nine.

In addition, the jail or prison population of most institutions is usually quite diverse. Chaplains must offer nondenominational worship services where particular doctrines are not forced upon the worshipers, and where inmates from all denominations and persuasions can gather in comfort. They may be able to assure this if they alone lead every worship service, but this is usually both impractical and undesirable. Bible studies, too, are not a vehicle for indoctrination; this is the role of the local church. Instead, Bible studies should offer hope and encouragement by focusing on Christ's grace and love and should provide spiritual resources for dealing successfully with daily problems the prisoner encounters.

Inevitably, worship services led by volunteer groups tend to take on identifiable characteristics of the host minister or sponsoring group. To combat this, chaplains must program for both variety and breadth; they should ensure that a wide range of groups with differing worship styles are included in the total program offerings, and they must also see that the churches conducting worship services are representative of the worship backgrounds of the existing inmate population.

For example, the chaplain of a facility composed of 55 percent African-American inmates is not programming for breadth if 90 percent of the worship services are conducted by Caucasians (see also Chapter Nine). Yet too many chaplains function as if the only characteristic of their congregation that matters is the fact that they are offenders. Of course, if any of these factors change, the chaplain should be prepared to adjust the institutional religious programs accordingly. Just as the changing demographics of a local church congregation demand new approaches to ministry, so any significant shifts in an inmate population, or changes in the institutional structure or mission may call for altering the worship or educational plan the chaplain has in place.

Having made the case for distinctions within the prison inmate community, I now want to argue for some commonality of that population. Though we minister to individuals, there is a common core of identifiable problems we can expect to find present in the lives of our parishioners. To ignore these would be foolish. Therefore, the Word of God that the chaplain delivers through a unified program of worship and study opportunities must speak to these issues. For instance, one of the worst aspects of prison life is the constant assault on the inmate's self-esteem, both from peers who see themselves as unworthy or unlovable rejects and from institutional staff whose actions and attitudes reinforce those feelings. A self-fulfilling prophesy is soon established: If an inmate perceives that he or she is worthless over a long enough period of time, that inmate comes to accept the evaluation and eventually begins to act out that internal belief. But through a careful study of Scripture, the prisoner learns he or she is acceptable—that a person's ultimate worth is not based on their own actions, but on Christ's. Then, through worship experiences, that same inmate draws closer to God, to self, and to his or her neighbor. Identifying with a community of the forgiven, the prisoner can begin to envision who he or she is in the eyes of Christ. This is the ultimate antidote for loss of self-esteem.

To be effective in the preaching and teaching of God's word, the institutional chaplain must have a thorough understanding of the dynamics at work in the lives of the men or women who inhabit that place. In addition to clearly identifiable institutional stress factors, there are several other characteristics present in the lives of many offenders that should be considered when developing the worship and educational programs of the chaplaincy. These are not environmental conditions or situational stresses that evolve within the prison setting; rather, these are historical, psychological, and social dynamics that exist in the offender's life prior to his or her incarceration and are then carried into the institution. Here, we will discuss just three of these factors, though there are more. The correctional chaplain should carefully consider any of these in developing sermon topics, planning Bible studies, and transmitting theological precepts that might be potentially effective agents of change in the lives of the men and women who are products of these circumstances.

First, inmate populations are **poorly educated** (formally). While the average IQ of prison inmates is only slightly below that of the general population, prisoners are distinct underachievers. According to the most recent data available from the *Bureau of Justice Statistics*, 40 percent of state prison inmates and 47 percent of jail inmates have failed to complete high school or its equivalent, which compares to 18 percent of the general population that fall into that category. Moreover, 14 percent of those State inmates and 13 percent of the jail inmates completed only the eighth grade or less. At the same time, a miniscule 2 to 3 percent of all inmates are college graduates. Federal inmates fare somewhat better, though they too are below national averages of the general population—only 27 percent of them fail to complete high school or its equivalent, and 8 percent of them are college graduates (Harlow 2003). This merely reflects the level of grade completed; it says nothing about their true level of functionality.

While there are many social implications to these figures, they also have conspicuous meaning for a chaplain structuring any strategic effort to provide access to God's Word inside correctional facilities. For one thing, people who comprise this demographic simply don't read well. In fact, they probably read very little. The average reading level of prison inmates is low: below the fifth grade in one study and below eighth grade in another. Nor are they likely skilled at processing intellectual and academic-based information.

In fact, research shows that 67 percent of prison inmates cannot write a brief letter explaining a billing error, read a map, or understand a bus schedule (Baer and Sabatini 17). Unfortunately, this contrasts with the primary information delivery system of the typical church, a model based on mental comprehension of religious principles discovered through a careful study of a collection of books—the Bible. Most men and women housed in institutions operate in quite different communication environments than that of the chaplain who serves them. To be effective, then, chaplains must adapt their strategies to align with this reality.

First, since a great many inmates are suspicious of any Bible translation other than the King James Version—the one they heard as a child and the one to which they ascribe most authority—the chaplain will find it beneficial to introduce and continually reinforce the use of more readable translations.

Second, worship services that are designed to invite participation are more likely to be beneficial than those that rely primarily on a one-way transmission of information through preaching. Music is a language that communicates outside the sphere of linear thinking, and will always strongly resonate with inmates.

Third, both in worship services and Bible studies, the leader should avoid complicated exegesis and sophisticated doctrinal concepts, concentrating instead on scriptural precepts that speak to basics where inmates live their lives each day. The messages and study need to focus on love, hope, the renewing of the mind, and on practical application of Scriptural texts.

There are other scenarios that will fit the circumstances described, and it is important to understand that this is not a discussion about any lack of intelligence or inability to learn. It concerns information processing styles, in the same manner that educators talk about the different processing styles of Baby Boomers (born 1946–64), Generation X (born 1965–77), and Generation Y (born after 1978). Successful chaplains must be adept at repackaging gospel truths in a form compatible with the learning characteristics of their hearers.

Not only are the majority of prisoners poorly educated, but they are also what I refer to as **religiously illiterate**. On my first chaplaincy assignment, I quickly learned that intake interviews provided opportunities to gain valuable information about my parishioners, so I designed a short form the inmate could complete, and that I could keep in my files. On the form, one of the questions asked for an indication of "religious preference." I soon noticed that an amazing number of my men checked the box for "Baptist." In my daily involvement with the inmates, however, I found little in the way of any systematic belief systems and only a vague sense of denominational design, so I began to suspect my intake document was faulty. Thinking perhaps the alphabetical listing skewed the selections in favor of Baptists, I rearranged the list. Still, the results remained nearly the same, so I began to question the inmates in more detail about their previous church affiliations. What I discovered provided me with a fundamental key to communicating with offender populations that has served me well throughout my career.

The institution I was serving at that time was located in the heart of the South—Atlanta—and there were large numbers of Baptist churches to choose from, especially in the inner city where most of my facility's prisoners grew up. I soon learned that often, in the early years of childhood, these men were faithfully taken to church by their mothers, grandmothers, or aunts (the father most often being absent). And that church was usually a Baptist one. With other men, I found that their predominant church experience centered on a one-week-per-year excursion to Vacation Bible School that, once again, most often took place in a nearby Baptist church. Thus, the fact that my men considered themselves "Baptist" had nothing to do with their understanding of doctrinal positions or church history; it merely illustrated that their repertoire of church experiences was severely limited. So instead of having a base of knowledge from which to decide their affiliation, they merely chose what was familiar.

This corroborates what we already know—most men and women experiencing criminal lifestyles are not heavily involved in churches. Furthermore, it underscores what I have referred to above as religious illiteracy. Most prisoners have an unsophisticated understanding of the vast majority of Biblical precepts. These beliefs are often a product of a few remembered Bible stories from their youth, combined with some sort of a deterministic view of life's realities as they perceive them, which are then filtered through a distorted view of an ultimate judge who oversees the world. All this is in contrast with the more mature faith leader who usually teaches and preaches to them from an academically based foundation. This is true in spite of the fact that chaplains and volunteer ministers are sometimes fooled by prisoners who are quite adept at parroting phraseology they have heard or read, but about which they know very little. Those who have effective chaplaincy programs pay attention to this illiteracy principle and design their offerings accordingly.

Those who have been caught in the web of crime most often exhibit serious **lifestyle handicaps**. The men and women whom God has entrusted to correctional chaplains often have serious social and psychological problems, as well as serious addictions that complicate their ability to receive God's word or to effectively respond to it. For instance, the typical offender comes from a single parent home that exhibited a high degree of conflict, abuse, and instability; over one-third have an immediate family member who has also been incarcerated; and nearly one-third of them report that their parent abused drugs or alcohol. Twelve percent of males were victims of either physical or sexual abuse in childhood, and for women, that statistic jumps to nearly 40 percent (see Gabel and Johnston 4–12). Growing up in such environments operates heavily against receiving any Gospel message that is presented in images of loving family relationships.

By way of illustration, imagine how difficult it is to relate the concept of a loving heavenly father to either a son who has known only a punishing father who beat him with regularity and provided little by way of encouragement, or to a young woman who has been sexually abused by a stepfather, live-in boyfriend, or another family member. On the other hand, prisoners seem quite ready to accept a harsh, vindictive God who resembles the authority figures they have encountered at home or within the criminal justice system. These are only two examples of a long list of complex problems dominating the lives of offenders to which chaplains must be sensitive, and which they must consider when framing any scriptural teaching.

One final insight will complete our discussion on this topic. Many Christians who have never been inside a correctional facility—and unfortunately, even some who volunteer there with regularity—think of prisons as dark dungeons where the Word of God never penetrates unless someone like them carries it in. The opposite is usually the case; the problem is not the absence of the Word but the presence of many contradictory messages, all claiming to be the only true Word. During the course of an average week, an inmate seeking to learn about God may watch a series of television evangelists, each with his distinct message carved to suit a particular agenda and packaged to appeal to a unique market share of the available audience. Then, that same inmate picks up a book someone passes along to him that enthusiastically presents some narrow view on a selected theological debate (a favorite topic is prophecy of end times, probably because it is so hard to dispute). Later that week, the prisoner may be cornered by one of his peers who has embraced a particular faith or adopted a specific creedal statement, who wants to proselytize his friend, and who assures him that only accepting their faith or perspective provides access to God. Then, over dinner, our prisoner listens to a conversation about New Age philosophy or some other cultic path his friends are wandering down.

In a confused state, this inmate now comes to a worship service or Bible study or pays a visit to the chaplain. What does that inmate receive in the service or study offered through the chaplaincy services of the institution? Is it yet another competing version of the truth? Does he receive another message that tries to be louder or more convincing or more appealing than the others? Or does the delivered Word of God somehow slice through the confusion and reach an untouched chord within the heart of our still-seeking prisoner? How does the chaplain respond to this questioning man or woman who asks for help in deciphering the mixture of messages? Does that chaplain offer a version that represents the doctrinal or denominational bias of the chaplain? Does the chaplain rely on a tract or handout that perhaps only offers yet another view of the argument? Or is the chaplain able to communicate the Word in ways that move the prisoner beyond a search for information *about* God to a discovery of a relationship with God? These are questions every chaplain should carefully consider.

There is a standard joke among prison and jail ministers about preaching to a "captive audience." Indeed, chaplains have a captive audience—a congregation that imports a complex set of personal problems into an institution organized and managed in ways that exacerbate stressors affecting that congregation. The setting provides a tremendous opportunity to present a healing, transforming message. As Ron Nickel, president of Prison Fellowship International, once remarked, "In the prison system, individual failure converges with societal failure, and from this there is no escape except through the Gospel" (Nickel). Whether or not the Gospel is presented in a way that liberates the hearer depends on the wisdom and spiritual discernment of the chaplain who coordinates the delivery of the worship and education programs within the institution.

MAINTAINING A MINISTRY OF PRESENCE WITHIN THE FACILITY

St. Francis of Assisi once called his friend Brother Juniper and said, "Come with me, Brother. Let's go out and preach to the people." Juniper went willingly, and they spent the day walking through towns and fields without saying a word. When they returned home, the puzzled Juniper said, "Father, all we did was walk around all day without saying a word. I thought we were going to preach to the people!" St. Francis answered, "Oh, but we did preach, Brother Juniper! As we walked, all the people saw us and that made them stop during their busy day and think of God!" And so it should be with the jail or prison chaplain who, even when not conducting a worship service, leading any religious program, or counseling a single inmate should nonetheless cause anyone he or she encounters in the institution to reflect on God. This cannot be learned from a textbook or even passed along through the wisdom of others; it is a character trait that is developed by God within the heart of those He chooses and calls into certain special ministry fields.

> *Often, our programs and counseling sessions have far less influence than does our coming alongside the broken people we serve and sharing their journey with them in an atmosphere of love and acceptance.*

For some prisoners, this ministry of presence may be all the chaplain offers that are of any real value. My early mentor told me it was sort of like sitting with your child who was in bed ill and running a high fever. You sat with the child, but often the sickness had to run its course, and there was nothing physically you could do to make it better. But somehow the sitting at the child's bedside and being there with the child had an effect—it made the condition easier to endure. To my mentor, this was one of the most valuable elements of pastoral ministry in the correctional setting, and through the years, I have come to accept his wisdom. Often, our programs and counseling sessions have far less influence than does our coming alongside the broken people we serve and sharing their journey with them in an atmosphere of love and acceptance.

Although precisely defining the ministry of presence is a difficult task, recognizing it when you see it is not. Twenty-five feet below its surface, the ocean is always tranquil. So, too, when I spend even a small amount of time with chaplains in their facilities, I can readily identify those whose ministry of presence has significantly impacted those places. In the midst of whatever turmoil, unrest, or negative energy that seems to be always present in the air of the jail or prison, the calming presence of the chaplain is clearly at work. If I can readily identify it during one of my infrequent visits, it is certain the institutional staff and inmates who encounter that chaplain daily are well aware of that sense of presence.

BUILDING RELATIONSHIPS WITH STAFF

Everyone who either works or lives in a jail or prison is affected by the institutional culture; if they don't resist its worst elements, they are eventually overcome by it. In most cases, correctional staff members are highly motivated individuals who are committed to public safety and who want to assist with the transformation of offenders. But at the same time, staff members of any institution are daily exposed to near lethal doses of the negativity, despair, violence, and cynicism that are bred on its premises. Prison may not be the end of the world, but one can easily see it from there, and although the staff can go home at the end of their shift, they too often carry some of the values and mindsets with them when they leave, thus infecting their own households. Multiple studies show that correctional officers in particular, like their law enforcement colleagues, are among the highest at-risk groups for spousal abuse and suicide, as well as exhibiting higher than average percentages of sleep disturbances, anger, PTSD and other co-occurring negative mental health symptoms.** Many of them have no pastors in the free world community, so for them the facility chaplain may be the only spiritual guide in their lives.

Chaplains make themselves available to staff when called upon, and they can enhance the probability of serving staff by intentionally setting out to cultivate relationships with them and by actively participating as members of the correctional team. Staff-responsive chaplains take the time to visit with staff as a part of their regular routines; they inquire about their families and listen to their personal stories; they provide counseling or make referrals when they uncover serious threats to their well-being;

and they offer to pray for them about those matters. Though the chaplain's formal job description often excludes this vital pastoral role, the chaplains should not compound that omission by rushing blindly past staff on their way to minister to the prisoner. A faithful ministry to staff will only improve the chaplain's ability to minister at every level within the facility and is really not optional. After all, the responsibilities of the "keeper of the cloak" extend to everyone within the perimeter of the institution.

Chaplains are not social workers, though the fact that each of the inmates they serve has been either accused or declared guilty of committing acts that violate societal norms. Nor are chaplains psychologists, even though much of their ministry efforts are in some way directed at helping inmates reconfigure their thinking. If they are to be effective in connecting with inmates who have a built-in resistance to those who represent the government responsible for their current incarceration, chaplains cannot be merely another counselor/advisor attempting to correct or control their behavior. Chaplains are first and foremost, shepherds who know their sheep and who are recognized by those sheep as men and women whose concern is for the daily welfare of the flock. The pastoral role is unique within the institution and cannot be assumed by anyone other than the chaplain. It is divinely ordained and must be carefully guarded.

*Two classic studies on the topic of prison culture are: Clemmer, Donald ([1940] 1958). *The Prison Community*. New York: Holt, Rinehart and Winston; and Sykes, Gresham M. (1958). *The Society of Captives: A Study of a Maximum Security Prison*. Princeton: Princeton University Press. Clemmer coined the term "prisonization" to describe the ways that inmates assimilate the social world of the prison and adapt to it. Sykes focused on the "pains of imprisonment"—deprivations that accompany the incarceration experience.

**An excellent supportive resource for correctional officers is: Desert Waters Correctional Outreach, http://desertwaters.com.)

REFERENCES

Baer, J., Kutner, M., and Sabatini, J. (2009). Basic Reading Skills and the Literacy of America's Least Literate Adults: Results from the 2003 National Assessment of Adult Literacy (NAAL) Supplemental Studies (NCES 2009–481). National Center for Education Statistics, Institute of Education Sciences, U.S. Department of Education. Wash., DC.

Gabel K and Johnston, D. eds. (1995). *Children of Incarcerated Inmates*. New York: Lexington Books.

Harlow, C. W. (2003) Education and Correctional Populations. Bureau of Justice Statistics (January). NCJ 195670.

Meador, Betty D. and Carl R. Rogers. (1984) Person-Centered Therapy. In *Current Psychotherapies*. 3rd ed. Raymond J. Corsini, ed. Itasca, IL: F. E. Peacock Publishers.

Nikkel, Ron. Address at Coalition of Prison Evangelists conference. Virginia Beach, VA: October 6, 1995.

Chapter Seven

Administrative Dimension

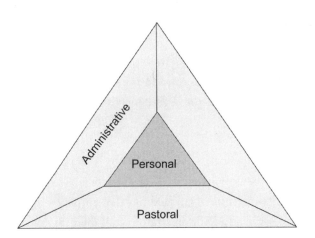

Historically, all discussions of correctional chaplaincy, whether they have taken place in textbooks, journal articles, or at training conferences, refer to the tasks of leading worship, supervising religious education, and counseling—the pastoral dimension of this ministry. More recently, as we have already documented, an evolution has taken place within the profession that prioritizes the program management aspect of the position. Many practitioners, however, see a fundamental conflict between the pastoral and administrative functions, and they often point to what they consider to be burdensome administrative duties every chaplain is required to perform at the expense of the "real" ministry to which he or she is called. These people find it difficult to view the work of administration in a positive light—at best it is considered a necessary evil.

Department of Corrections administrators in at least one state apparently agree with the philosophical premise of this distinction. Colorado utilizes privately funded chaplains who are in turn managed by several regional coordinators from the DOC's *Office of Faith and Citizen Programs*. The pivotal philosophical position expressed by Colorado officials in support of this arrangement is the notion that the role of the state is to ensure that the inmate's religious rights are fairly administered, while the role the community of faith is to minister to those inmates who choose to follow a particular religious path. Virginia's position is similar. There, chaplains have never been employed by the state, on the basis that it would be a violation of the separation of Church and State, and chaplains are procured through designated service providers representative of different faith traditions.

> *Organizing, structuring, and implementing programs are administrative functions, and to the degree a chaplain is effective in these tasks is the degree to which religious programs will be effective.*

Nonetheless, the dominant model in state correctional facilities, as well as in those county or regional jail facilities that employ chaplains, calls for the chaplain to serve as an administrator of all the programs and services that flow from that office. I encourage chaplains to see this as a ministry— not a drudgery. Indiscriminate religious programs that are not organized to meet the wide range of inmate needs, nor designed in a way that nurtures them throughout their faith journey will probably fail to effect meaningful change in their lives.

Organizing, structuring, and implementing programs are administrative functions, and to the degree a chaplain is effective in these tasks is the degree to which religious programs will be effective. This is not to say that some individual program on which the chaplain focuses and for which he or she is uniquely gifted will not be highly successful. That success, however, does not negate two important facts. First, a broad, multifaceted program using a variety of strategies and modalities is necessary to reach the difficult and diverse population within a correctional facility. Chaplains who are content with one effective program type and who fail to understand the need for multiple strategies are limiting God's channels for change in the institution. Second, every program offering can benefit from a strong administrative touch; good programs, carefully managed, will get even better.

Here, it is important to understand the distinction between the term *chaplain* and *chaplaincy*. Sometimes, chaplains get out of balance and make their ministry all about themselves, becoming both the message and the vehicle through which that message is transmitted. What we should understand is that to adequately and effectively minister to the wide variety of needs contained within the correctional population it is necessary to offer a full range of program options—what we might call a "suite of services". The chaplain (a person) is the one who must design, implement, and monitor this complementary group of services and delivery options (the chaplaincy) available within the facility. This is also an important distinction for administrators to grasp. Having a person duly designated as the facility chaplain may meet someone's definition of supplying minimal religious services, but that in no way equates with having a vibrant chaplaincy.

DEVELOPING AND MAINTAINING AN INSTITUTIONAL MINISTRY PLAN

The administrative process should reflect clear strategic planning. That begins with a careful analysis of the institutional mission to determine precisely where faith-based programs and pastoral services align with it and what specific sorts of offerings will best match the expressed values and goals of that mission. One size, model, or brand of chaplaincy services simply does not fit all settings. Differing goals call for differing ministry programs and/or pastoral approaches.

The next step is to identify the demographics of the inmate population—age, gender, nature of offense, security classification, specialized behavioral designations, etc. Normally, the population characteristics closely parallel the mission of the facility, though in many cases prisons will have a broad range of inmate profiles and treatment classifications distributed across different housing units within the institution. Jails, on the other hand, since they are primarily temporary holding facilities serving localized communities, seldom house discrete demographic populations. A clear exception might be certain federal detention centers designed to hold specialized groups of offenders such as Immigration and Customs Enforcement (ICE) detainees.

After determining what the mission is and who the residents are, chaplains must then consider how any prominent physical features of the correctional institution may impact program facilitation. Some environments lend themselves to certain ministry models, while other designs may create significant barriers to particular types of ministry efforts. Here too, the specific institutional mission and inmate population usually correlate with the physical characteristics of the design. In prisons, higher security needs normally means restricted spaces and minimal movement of inmates; similarly, jail designs seldom have extensive designated program areas. Such factors play a major role in the development of any well-conceived chaplaincy plan.

The point is that few things in the chaplain's routine should take place outside an overall operational plan; even spontaneous ministry opportunities can emerge from within a structured framework that permits and encourages such events. In the same way, no item on the calendar of religious activities should be randomly selected; all events should be directed at meeting identified needs within a specific setting. Clearly, these two principles will only prove true if the chaplain deliberately prepares, monitors, and maintains a ministry plan that is designed for the specific institution in which he or she serves. We will leave the full discussion of this topic for Chapter Nine.

DEVELOPING VOLUNTEERS: RECRUITING, TRAINING, SUPERVISING/ASSESSING

Administratively speaking, there is a considerable amount of paperwork attached to the everyday management of religious services—lists of activities to distribute, inmate requests to process, documentation to be made in inmate files, and reports of all kinds to complete. However, the most time-consuming administrative duty, and often the most critical to the success of chaplaincy programming, is the coordination of religious volunteers (in many facilities, chaplains serve as coordinators of *all* volunteer services).

Not all correctional officials, or even all chaplains for that matter, see volunteers as necessary or desirable. As one of my colleagues once remarked, "I can do it better; volunteers are too slow; and they don't do it the way I wanted it done in the first place!" Those who distrust the heavy use of volunteers in the institution often believe they lack essential training, increase staff workloads, create potentially dangerous situations, or even threaten job security. However, when strategically deployed and effectively managed by a competent chaplain, volunteers form an essential and even vital component of a successful chaplaincy program for a number of reasons:

- The enormity of the job chaplains are asked to perform requires additional helpers.
- Volunteers come with an assortment of gifts and skills that both complement and enhance the ministry of the chaplain.
- Volunteers link prisoners to the "free-world," reminding them that they are still a part of that community.
- Visitors from the outside incarnate the word of God; they are the embodiment of Christ to the inmates they meet (a corollary of *Matthew 25:31–46*).

Some initial decisions must be made regarding the number of volunteers needed to fulfill program requirements and what qualifications each should have. Placing the right person in the appropriate position is crucial. Too often, chaplains work to merely fill slots in the schedule, rather than to locate an individual who is prompted to serve by the Holy Spirit and well-qualified to lead or support a particular program. A chaplain is probably better off to cancel a program than to entrust it to someone who will not be effective.

The management of volunteers consists of three basic components: recruitment; training; and supervision/assessment. We will briefly discuss each of these, recognizing that there is much more to this area of expertise than can be adequately covered in a single chapter.

Recruitment

Generally speaking, if the security requirements of an institution are appropriate for the use of volunteers and institutional officials support their involvement, chaplains will not have to work hard to recruit volunteers from the faith community. They will approach the chaplain unsolicited. That is not always a positive situation, however, for faith-based volunteers come to institutions with a variety of agendas, some of which are inconsistent with the program developed by the chaplain. The desire to be a volunteer doesn't necessarily qualify one for that role; chaplains should turn down any person or organization not suitable for the designated plan or unwilling to adjust to it and do so without any feeling of guilt.

It is especially important that religious volunteers are capable of working within the unique multifaith environment of corrections. To a certain degree, training can prepare them for this adjustment, but there are individuals whose religious convictions or zealousness for their own doctrines prevent them from conforming to the necessary demeanor this ministry demands. That is true not only of those who don't respect religions other than their own, but also of those who feel compelled to force their specific doctrinal beliefs on others within their own faith.

> *Without question, the most critical part of volunteer management is training. While this is often limited to what takes place prior to a work assignment, training should be an ongoing, continuous process that offers support for the volunteer, while at the same time providing quality control*

When it does become necessary for the chaplain to seek volunteer workers, the first point of contact should be any current volunteer worker who is performing satisfactorily. The next step, of course, is for the chaplain to contact area churches and ask for opportunities to share from the pulpit or to meet with small interest groups. In scheduling churches to lead worship services, most chaplains like to rotate them either monthly or quarterly, depending on interest and the extent of open dates. There are chaplains, of course, who feel strongly that they alone should be in the chapel pulpit every Sunday when possible. Still others believe it is more important to have inmates connected to congregations of believers from the larger community of faith that transcends the jail or prison walls. Group studies, on the other hand, call for volunteers that are able to commit to long-term leadership roles. The need for multiple religious education offerings covering a variety of topics also means that there is a greater demand for these talented individuals.

Believers who respond to an invitation to serve in correctional settings will do so, of course, from the perspective of their faith—they believe deeply that they are their brother's keeper, and that they should give of themselves to help others. However, that doesn't preclude other altruistic reasons for seeking volunteering. An awareness of some of these other, more personal reasons will help the chaplain manage religious programs more effectively and develop better working relationships with these nonpaid assistants. Some of the motivations for volunteering include:

- A chance to use special knowledge and skills that are not employed in other life activities.
- The desire to contribute to the community in which one lives.
- The belief that one's involvement can make a difference in the world.
- The opportunity to do something new and exciting.
- The need to feel useful or important.
- A way to pay back for similar help one has received in the past.

Careful screening through interviews can identify these and other reasons for desiring to serve as volunteers, each of which has some merit and may exist alongside those motivations tied more directly to the person's faith. Understanding these desires and needs for personal gratification helps the chaplain in two ways. First, it aids him or her in recruiting efforts; second, it helps retention of good volunteers as the chaplain uses the information to keep volunteers feeling important, successful, and content as they continue their efforts.

Training

Without question, the most critical part of volunteer management is training. While this is often limited to what takes place prior to a work assignment, training should be an ongoing, continuous process that offers support for the volunteer, while at the same time providing quality control. The first phase of training should be an orientation that introduces new volunteers to the institution, provides insights into the inmate population, and reviews the breadth of chaplaincy services. A second phase should offer specific training for the program with which individual volunteers or groups will be working. It may also be helpful to conduct periodic sessions covering topics of general interest that all religious program volunteers attend. In the prisons where I served, we made quarterly training available and required all volunteers to attend a minimal number of sessions each year to maintain their active status. Ongoing training events not only allow for quality control, they also provide fellowship and help individual workers understand their part in the total chaplaincy effort. The final phase is a form of continuing education we will discuss under the **supervision and assessment** category below.

Volunteer orientation in some jails and prisons often consists entirely of a member of the security team reciting a list of inmate games, accompanied by stories of volunteers who were fooled—to everyone's detriment—and ending with a display of confiscated weapons and other contraband items. This is designed to alert trainees to the dangers of the institution where they will be working and to impress upon them the necessity of security measures, which are important concerns. Unfortunately, rather than creating a team atmosphere where the chaplain and volunteers join hands to work together toward common goals, this approach often serves more as a point of polarization, emphasizing a "them-versus-us" mentality and subtly coercing volunteers to choose a side—inmate or staff. Although a reasonable part of orientation should focus on institutional rules and potential problems of working with offenders, my strong conviction is that it is critical the initial session should concentrate on positive aspects of the ministry programs and establish a tone of expectation that God will work through those programs to produce fruit. In addition, the procedural aspects of delivering institutional programs should be covered at that session: signing into the facility, time constraints, volunteer time sheets, etc.

Depending on the nature of the program, a second phase—specific task or skills training—may be offered individually or in a group setting.

For instance, although chaplains will not offer a homiletics course for ministers who lead worship services, they should offer insights from their own experiences, discuss certain topics to avoid, explain guidelines for worship expressions, and establish a baseline of clear expectations. Similar discussions should cover Bible studies and other group activities, counseling sessions, or individual mentorships. The chaplain is God's appointed pastor in the institution, charged with shepherding the flock. It is also the chaplain who has experience working in corrections and has fashioned an integrated program designed to intervene in the lives of prisoners and affirm their faith journeys. Therefore, no chaplain should ever simply turn over an activity to ministering individuals or church groups to do as they please; rather the chaplain should set the parameters for each activity in accordance with his or her overall program objectives and the institutional policies and procedures.

Supervision and Assessment

Often, programs and the volunteers who lead them become permanent fixtures in the schedule of religious activities, not because they have proven effective, but merely because they are not monitored. With no basis for judging the merit of the activity or its leadership, unless some obvious problem arises, the chaplain simply assumes that "no news is good news" and allows the program to continue indefinitely. This practice is inexcusable. Any religious program worth initiating is worth assessing; any volunteer competent to lead a program will only improve when adequately supervised and correctly evaluated.

Supervision and assessment begin with development of two written documents: a program definition and a volunteer job description. The first is roughly equivalent to a mission statement, expressing overall goals and objectives of the program. The latter document becomes a contract of sorts, identifying the specific functions the volunteer agrees to perform. Both these instruments become tools for accountability the chaplain uses to determine how well the volunteer is performing (supervision) and how well the program is achieving the desired results (assessment). The program definition is formulated by the chaplain prior to recruiting a leader; indeed, the definition dictates some of the leader's qualifications and the commitments he or she will need to make. On the other hand, parts of the job description may be worked out jointly by the chaplain and prospective volunteer. In this way, the volunteer has some ownership of the agreement to which he or she is committing.

Every program—even those with the most obvious objectives—should have a written definition, and every volunteer—even those whose duties are most simple—should have a written job description. Samples of both documents, used in a prison mentoring program conducted in two institutions where I worked as chaplain, are provided here for analysis. These are rather simple documents, and many correctional systems use far more detailed instruments, but these will serve as useful models. Written in an uncomplicated style, they deliberately steer clear of stiff, academic language and the formalized behavioral objectives favored by many social scientists. Each chaplain can create documents that fit with his or her particular approach, as long as the principles are maintained.

FAITH-BASED COMMUNITY MENTOR

Program Description

This is a unique ministry program that has the potential to motivate truly lasting and meaningful effects on the lives of individuals. It goes beyond the more traditional forms of ministry such as Bible study, literature distribution, and musical programs to a ministry of sharing personal experiences in Christ. This approach is designed to not only tell inmates about God's love, but to actually show them that love in action.

In the Faith-Based Mentoring Program, a Christian man, woman, or couple attempts to form a lasting, loving Christian relationship with an inmate. This relationship begins with the person or couple sharing with the inmate for an hour or two every week or so. While the relationship begins in prison, it is anticipated that the Christian person or couple act as a sort of sponsor once the inmate is released, helping him or her with readjustment to the "free world", and particularly with finding a permanent church home.

The program requires a serious, long-term commitment. Even though the inmates involved have requested to participate in the program, establishing a truly loving Christian relationship with them is likely to be difficult. Many inmates have never experienced true Christian love, a love that gets even stronger when someone is most unlovable. The first time they experience this love, inmates often find it unbelievable and somewhat frightening. Therefore, they are likely to test its limits, and thus test the volunteer's commitment to the program. Developing a loving Christian relation

ship with an inmate is likely to be a lengthy and difficult process, but the rewards are great.

Program Objectives
1. Discover real rather than perceived needs.
2. Build the inmate's self-esteem.
3. Help him/her deal realistically with guilt.
4. Let the inmate know he/she is loved unconditionally.
5. Present positive future lifestyle alternatives.
6. Encourage him/her to take responsibility for their actions.
7. Witness through example.

VOLUNTEER JOB DESCRIPTION

TITLE: Faith-Based Community Mentor

Major Objectives:
To assist inmate to achieve healthy self-concepts; to provide support system for inmate; to assist the Chaplaincy Services Department with any specific goals for the inmate; to assist in inmate's spiritual/religious growth.

Major Responsibilities:

To visit assigned inmate on a predetermined regular basis; to provide support for inmate through the development of a personal relationship; to supply Chaplaincy Services Department with periodic progress reports.

Qualifications:

Eighteen (18) years of age or older, sincere desire to counsel on a personal basis, recommendations through local church or prison ministry, prescreening through the sending church or community-based ministry organization.

Training and/or Preparations:

The Chaplaincy Services Department will provide orientation and required periodic training (usually once per quarter), group and individual sessions.

Time and Place:

To be arranged through Chaplaincy Services Department.

Commitment:

Long-term extended time commitment (usually no less than six months) and consistent performance of responsibilities (to include attendance at training sessions).

Supervision:

By the Chaplaincy Services Department and other designated institutional staff.

Additional Individual Requirements:

Date:_____

_____

Volunteer Signature

_____

Chaplain's Signature

Once programs are underway and volunteers assigned, ongoing supervision and evaluation should proceed systematically to assess both the procedures and outcomes of the activities. The following guidelines should prove effective in implementing this process.

- Chaplains should occasionally sit in on worship services, Bible studies, and any other group activity. Weekly activities might be visited quarterly; those that meet monthly might be observed semiannually. Some institutional polices require this monitoring.
- In all cases, volunteers should be required to submit periodic written reports. Once again, a quarterly report is a reasonable expectation. Here, too, some systems have established reporting mechanisms already in place.
- The chaplain and volunteer should meet to discuss the written report for the purposes of assessing how well program objectives are being met and the volunteer is functioning.
- The chaplain should affirm positive aspects of the program and acknowledge the volunteer's role in the total institutional program.
- When deficiencies are identified, the chaplain and volunteer should jointly develop strategies for improvement.
- Program objectives or volunteer job descriptions should be revised, as needed, to accommodate changing realities or expectations.

If a program doesn't deliver the intended result or has outlived its usefulness, the chaplain should not hesitate to eliminate it and make room on the schedule for something more productive. If a volunteer demonstrates an inability to successfully direct the activity to which he or she is assigned, the chaplain needs to terminate the relationship. Maintaining poorly functioning programs or keeping ineffective volunteers in place, regardless of their length of service, isn't good practice.

Volunteers are an extremely valuable resource—available, willing, and capable of helping the chaplain deliver spiritual solutions to prisoners searching for alternatives to their destructive life patterns. They arrive as representatives from the communities that the prisoner has offended, model successful social and faith-driven behaviors, and offer acceptance and forgiveness. Moreover, volunteers are responding directly to the scriptural mandate to "remember those in prison" (*Hebrews 13:3*), and expect to find the image of God buried somewhere in the lives of those they visit (*Matthew 25:31–46*). The administration of an effective volunteer program is clearly one of the important ministries the correctional chaplain performs. *

INTERFACING WITH MINISTRY ORGANIZATION LEADERSHIP

In most instances, chaplains are required to provide periodic reports to their sponsoring agency, whether that is a unit within their denominational affiliation, an administrator of a private corporation, a nonprofit ministry board, or—in a few cases—an individual church congregation. Not only do these reports serve as vehicles of accountability, but they also provide opportunities to share information about the work God is doing in the jails or prisons with those individuals in influential positions who are not always well-versed in the world in which the chaplain lives. Rather than seeing this obligatory report as a time-consuming diversion from ministry activities, the wise chaplain creates a well-crafted document that has the potential to attract support from the organizational leadership. If such a report is not mandated, or if only a cursory version is acceptable, the chaplain should go above and beyond the minimal requirements to produce a moving and informative document.

In addition to any required reporting mechanism, the chaplain should communicate significant accomplishments with regularity as a way of educating the segment of the Church community that seldom understands and often conveniently ignores the marginalized population found within our nation's correctional facilities. In almost every instance where chaplaincy positions have been threatened by legislative actions, informed church and faith-based communities have been instrumental in salvaging at least some of the embattled territory. On the other hand, when too few people know the full details of what God accomplishes through the delivery of effective correctional ministry, chaplains cannot expect supportive assistance. Chaplains need to tell their stories, and the ministry organization with which they are affiliated is the most easily accessible and potentially influential audience.

INTERFACING WITH INSTITUTIONAL LEADERSHIP

Obviously, it is critical for the chaplain to have a strong working relationship with the senior administrative team of the correctional facility. When a warden or superintendent appreciates the value of religious programs, this relationship is relatively easy for a high- functioning chaplain to maintain; when that top jail or prison administrator is insensitive to or even neutral about chaplaincy services, the task is much harder. This is where the relational skills of the chaplain are challenged! Sometimes chaplains are content to work in tiny corners, often believing that keeping a low profile is the best policy. I advocate just the opposite. Chaplains should identify precisely where they appear on the organizational chart and then become fully engaged with institutional activities at that juncture.

Even if that placement is less desirable than the chaplain would hope for, he or she should remember that within organizations influence is not always a product of hierarchical placement. Chaplains should intentionally strive to add value to the overall operation of the institution in any way open to them. Attending shift meetings can be beneficial; it establishes presence, enhances communication with the line staff, and demonstrates that the chaplain cares about the full breadth of institutional concerns—not just those people and activities under the banner of religion. Establishing periodic meeting times with the warden or jail administrator—not just with the immediate program supervisor—is vital. These provide occasions for the chaplain to offer assistance with appropriate institutional goals, suggest training modules in an area of his or her expertise, and demonstrate concern and availability to staff members. Chaplains should also advocate for a position on the institution's emergency response team, even if it is merely serving coffee to the correctional staff. The ultimate goal of all this is to become such an asset to the institution that administrators would find it hard to do without the chaplain's involvement. But this is not a plan for job stability; it is a prescription for service that brings honor to our Lord!

Chaplains are called to serve everyone within the institution, while being owned by no one but God. In fulfilling the functions of their position, they must wear many hats. Some hats can be chosen, but others are forced upon the chaplain by administrative fiat. If the hat a chaplain chooses is at odds with administrative expectations, the chaplain's ability to have free rein over his or her program area will be diminished. At the very least, chaplains may experience some form of "punishment" by top level institutional officials during the course of their daily activities. On the other hand, choosing a position that parallels administrative concerns, but which is in opposition to inmate expectations, often alienates the chaplain from them.

There are two specific ways the chief administrator of an institution effectively neutralizes a chaplain. First, the administrator may figuratively put his or her arm around the chaplain and identify him or her as "My chaplain." This places the chaplain thoroughly on the side of prison administrative staff and makes it extremely difficult to effectively minister among the inmate population.

A second neutralization takes place when the administrator treats religious programs as unimportant and positions the chaplain as a second-class staff person, unworthy of offering serious input into the operations of the institution. This potentially nullifies any positive outcome of those programs the chaplain coordinates. The correctional chaplain must walk a tightrope between the keepers and the kept, taking sides with neither and pledging allegiance to God alone. Tightrope walking takes both skill (gifts, seasoned with training and experience) and balance (spiritual maturity).

FACILITATING ALL RECOGNIZED FAITH GROUPS

There are a number of tasks an institutional chaplain will be required to perform that may not be consistent with the tenants of that chaplain's particular faith. Within the administrative dimension of the position, that means facilitating the needs of inmates who embrace a religion other than their own. For instance, during the month of Ramadan, the holy month of fasting ordained by the Koran, the chaplain must make arrangements with the institutional food services supervisor for special meals to be served to Islamic inmates during the evening hours. Some Jewish inmates may partake only of a kosher diet throughout their period of incarceration. Native Americans may want access to a sweat lodge on the prison grounds. There are religious medals, pieces of clothing, and other sacred items associated with various religions that may require special administrative processes that demand the chaplain's involvement, oversight, and faithful attention.

For some Christian jail or prison ministers, this presents a dilemma. They consider this aspect of chaplaincy to be in conflict with the tenets of their faith since these sorts of duties not only don't serve to advance the cause of Christ, the act of performing them is construed as actively working against that cause. A few of these ministers, therefore, simply refuse to serve as institutional chaplains, confining their efforts to delivering specifically Christian programs from a base outside the institutional structure. I respect the sincerity of these individuals and don't judge their convictions. At the same time, we must recognize that the First Amendment of the U.S. Constitution guarantees the right to freedom of religion. Most recent in a long line of significant court decisions is that of *Cutter v Wilkinson* (2005) in which the U.S. Supreme Court upheld the Religious Land Use and Institutionalized Persons Act (RLUIPA) which stipulates that prisons must accommodate the religious practices of all recognized faiths without partiality. To the correctional chaplain falls the task of implementing religious accommodations that are consistent with the law of the land. They are responsible for facilitating the spiritual needs of all inmates—not just those who accept the principles of the chaplain's faith. Not only should this offer no barriers to effective ministry, it may well provide new opportunities for service.

Several years ago, I was conducting research on chaplaincy in a large prison in a western state, and one aspect of that called for a colleague and me to interview a group of inmates about the services they received in their facility. We deliberately structured the interviews so inmates from several religions participated—there was a Muslim in the group, a Native American, a Wiccan, and two Christian inmates. We talked for more than an hour about the way chaplaincy programs functioned in their institution and discussed specific details of how their chaplain facilitated various aspects of their programs. For most of the time, the Native American was quiet, though on two occasions he expressed frustration with the administration of the facility and what he considered their foot-dragging with respect to providing a sweat lodge in an acceptable location on prison grounds. When I asked about the role of the chaplain in that effort, he stated that he had not dealt with the chaplain, choosing instead to work through the volunteer coordinator and deputy warden's offices.

As the meeting progressed, the Muslim inmate, in particular, offered high praise of his Christian chaplain. He mentioned how carefully the chaplain rearranged religious icons and pictures within the chapel in a way that provided neutral space for the Friday Jum'ah prayer service. He also described, at length, how the chaplain had gone out of his way to assist the inmate in making arrangements for his mother's funeral and then followed up by checking on his well-being in the days immediately following. After hearing several of these stories, the Native American inmate who had been silent for most of the session voluntarily interjected, "I think the next time I have a problem, I'm going to come to the chaplain for help instead of going to the volunteer coordinator." Clearly, the witness projected by that chaplain was profound, and his ministry evidenced by virtue of his loving behavior!

> *In my* **administrative role,** *I facilitate any faith; but in my* pastoral role, *I serve those who either share my faith or choose to ask my counsel on the basis of that faith. I am not required to relinquish my pastoral identity to be faithful either to the law of the land or the law of love to which I want to be faithful.*

There are some chaplaincy spokespersons who attempt to challenge the ability of those chaplains whom they consider to be too zealous for Christ—too evangelical, perhaps. Most of these critics are dedicated to a model of chaplaincy that offers a generic or hybrid brand of spirituality whereby the chaplain lays no claim to his or her particular faith and who easily finds some truth in all religion. I strongly resist this approach, and specifically reject any notion that a chaplain is somewhat suspect unless he or she adopts such a posture. If I become merely a neutral conduit through whom any and all faiths flow—someone who only offers some sort of sacred hospitality—then what do I have to offer any inmate who asks me to share from my faith? Nothing than what any secular counselor might have to offer. Aquinas tells us that action follows upon being, and that we cannot give what we do not possess; so if I have nothing to offer from the repository of my faith, then my pastoral role is substantially diminished.

Here is the critical distinction on which this dilemma is resolved: In my administrative role, I facilitate any faith; but in my pastoral role, I serve those who either share my faith or choose to ask my counsel on the basis of that faith. I am not required to relinquish my pastoral identity to be faithful either to the law of the land or the law of love to which I want to be faithful. Assisting inmates in exercising their constitutional rights is clearly an administrative dimension of the chaplaincy, and one any chaplain can easily fulfill on those terms, apart from any pastoral entanglements.

A foundational truth about Christ is that He loved and served everyone, while condemning no one; He simply bore witness to the Truth. The Christian chaplain emulates Him by serving all inmates (including nonbelievers) without prejudice, and then trusting in his or her personal walk and institutional witness to express that faith. Indeed, as I understand it, my Christian faith compels me to act in such a way—it is a natural extension of who I am. Along the way, I have found many opportunities to minister to men and women of different faiths and have done so in the name and Spirit of my Master.

With this discussion of the administrative dimension of chaplaincy, we declare an axiom: If God calls a person to be an institutional chaplain, He is also calling that person to administer an entire program of chaplaincy services, for which He will provide appropriate gifting (see *I Corinthians 12:28*). Chaplains should embrace the idea that administrative chores are acts of ministry, and if they feel inadequate to meet the challenge, rejoice in the prospect of mastering some new skills or adding additional members to the team. We should also stipulate the converse of this principle: If a minister truly believes that God wants him or her to concentrate solely in a specialized ministry area and feels led to avoid administrative tasks, then God is not leading that minister into a position as institutional chaplain. Fulfilling the demands of the position clearly calls for strong administrative oversight.

*The one must-read for every volunteer is: Spitale, Lennie. (2002). *Prison Ministry: Understanding Prison Culture Inside and Out*. Nashville, TN: B&H Publishing Group.

REFERENCES

Cutter v. Wilkinson, 544 U.S. 709 (2005)

Chapter Eight

Community Dimension

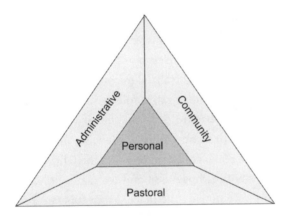

Thus far, we have examined the role of a chaplain within the confines of the institution itself. If we adhered to a strict definition of *institutional chaplain*, we would argue that a chaplain's responsibilities end at the front gate of the correctional facility. Many chaplains and the correctional systems they serve adopt this stance and deny the appropriateness of any ministry role not directly related to the staff or inmates within their assigned institution. In many instances, there are even strict policies forbidding the chaplain to have any contact with inmates after their release. While there is some wisdom in this approach, there are also many good reasons for chaplains to have at least some controlled interactions with ex-offenders or those community-based resource providers assisting the inmate with reentry to the free world. For one thing, chaplains have considerable knowledge about the inmate's spiritual strength—an important element in that prisoner's agenda for success. For another, the chaplain should have meaningful connections with the larger community of faith, and will be able to readily access supportive relationships that are so crucial in the reentry process.

If, however, chaplains isolate themselves from the larger community of believers, then they lose the opportunity to incorporate the body of Christ into a work to which that community has been specifically called. In an era when society is embracing increasingly harsh punishments for offenders and commonly rejecting any notion that people are redeemable, the prison chaplain stands in a singularly strategic position to speak prophetically to the Church in the local community. Many chaplains can have wonderfully effective ministries, but if those efforts take place entirely in isolation, outside the context of a larger picture, that work remains incomplete. Chaplains should see themselves as part of the larger Church that has assigned them to serve in a specialized ministry within the correctional institution. Although the administrative role as facility chaplain is to develop and manage a volunteer base to serve that facility, the natural extension of that role converges with a community dimension. In the larger scheme of things, chaplains are really collaborating with the Church to assist with the spiritual development of those men and women who will likely one day rejoin the community outside the fence. From this perspective, chaplains are but one part of a continuum of services; one element in the total fabric of pastoral services by the Church to people with specialized needs.

FOSTERING COMMUNITY AWARENESS AND PARTNERSHIPS

Unfortunately, promoting a ministry to offenders does not produce many supporters, even in Christ's Church. The story of Jesus' return to his hometown recorded in Luke 4:14–30 provides an interesting parallel to what many of us who attempt to sensitize the Christian community to the cause of correctional ministry experience all too frequently. The story is set in the beginning of Jesus' ministry, but He had already aroused a good bit of interest among the citizens through His performance of some early miracles. When He returned to His home town, His reputation had preceded Him, so that upon His arrival at the synagogue on the Sabbath, He was invited to participate in the service.

On that day, Jesus read a passage from the prophet Isaiah that focused on the ministry of the promised Messiah, a message of good news to, among others, the prisoners (*vs. 18*). When He sat down, He gazed intently at His audience and proclaimed, "Today this scripture is fulfilled in your hearing" (*vs. 21, NIV*). Although it is true that with these words Jesus was declaring He was the long-awaited Messiah, He was also identifying a particular characteristic of His ministry—that it was directed to the poor, the prisoner, the oppressed of society, and not just a select in-crowd who claimed a special heritage from God. And while His hearers that day were initially open to the idea that Jesus just might be the anointed one of God, they were decidedly unwilling to accept the radical nature of the ministry He portrayed.

So Jesus made it a little clearer. In fact, He illustrated His ministry in such a way that the Jewish listeners could not help but understand His message. First, He pointed out that prophets were never accepted in their hometowns. Then, using stories from the very prophets his listeners revered, Jesus reminded those present that day that on two critical occasions it was Gentiles, rather than Jews, who were favored by God, because the Gentiles were the ones who had been receptive to the ministry of His servants (*vs. 24–27*). Upon hearing this, the crowd in the synagogue became so enraged that they would have killed Jesus had it not been for divine intervention (*vs. 28–30*).

> *Chaplains should see themselves as extensions of the Christian community, working in places of confinement to reconcile and restore offenders with the community-at-large. Their work has no purpose and no direction if it is carried on without the support and participation of churches in the community.*

In today's Church, a large portion of those who consider themselves Christians resemble those Jews gathered in the synagogue that day; they consider themselves to be fully devoted disciples of Christ, yet they reject the full ramifications of the Gospel message. Trapped into a works mentality, many Christians cannot quite grasp the expansiveness of God's grace, which is broad enough to embrace even the vilest of offenders. All of us are inclined to sympathize with the logic of a doctrine of works; after all, Scripture calls people to live righteously, to love their neighbors, and to be peacemakers in the world. We want to believe that if we accept Christ as Savior and try hard to fulfill His commandments, then rewards will be ours on the basis of merit. On the other hand, those who fail to live up to this standard "deserve" to be condemned. This mentality, which permeates the Church, is a particular stumbling block to appreciating any ministry to offenders, and that fact is what underscores the necessity for the correctional chaplain to bring a prophetic voice to the community of believers. The sacrificial work of chaplains inside the walls of our nation's jails and prisons continues to yield poor harvests, at least partly because the Church is not equally committed to the labor.

Chaplains are ideally qualified to help motivate local churches on these matters, but they don't always accept this part of their call. Many chaplains are so involved with the work of their particular institutions that they seldom even participate in a local church within their community, a point we touched on in an earlier chapter. This is a serious omission. Not being a part of a local congregation isolates the chaplain from a vital base of needed support and understanding for correctional ministry. A ministry to offenders and their families is far too large and much too complex to be adequately handled only by professionals functioning inside the institution. Chaplains should see themselves as extensions of the Christian community, working in places of confinement to reconcile and restore offenders with the community-at-large. Their work has no purpose and no direction if it is carried on without the support and participation of churches in the community. If a partnership between the Church and the institution doesn't exist, the chaplain must work to create one.

Chaplains often complain about the lack of interest in correctional ministry among local churches and community groups, especially in the area of available resources for ex-offenders and their families. However, the chaplain must make him or herself a vital part of the solution by encouraging the development of such resources in communities adjacent to the prison, as well as on a larger scale. The chaplain can use speaking opportunities to sensitize churches to the difficulties experienced by families of the incarcerated or by newly released offenders, and to stimulate enthusiasm for developing or expanding community resources. It is becoming clear that, as public institutions move to distance themselves from any appearance of religious alignments, a critical function of chaplaincy in the future will be the ability to initiate and maintain active partnerships with local churches and faith-based organizations.

EDUCATING THE CHURCH AND COMMUNITY ABOUT JUSTICE MINISTRIES

Although a large portion of the Church will not be sympathetic to a ministry among society's outcasts, there is a small but enthusiastic group of Christians scattered throughout the Church who respond to Christ's call to visit and witness to prisoners. As we discussed in Chapter Seven, these people are invaluable resources the chaplain should cultivate and equip for partnership in the institutional ministry. But the chaplain's prophetic ministry must also be directed toward doing more than merely managing these human resources as a volunteer labor pool; the chaplain should channel these co-ministers into those areas of ministry that have the highest potential to change lives and then implement training experiences that will prepare them to function effectively.

Chaplains must accept, as a legitimate part of their ministry, the role of educating the local church and reshaping or redirecting its ministry impulses into activities that include offenders, their families, victims of crime, and at-risk populations in general.

To cite but one example: representatives from the faith community who become interested in correctional ministry usually start off thinking of the jail or prison as a dark dungeon, devoid of the Word of God, which must then be invaded and taken for the cause of Christ. They also tend to favor evangelistic approaches, concentrating primarily on winning souls rather than serving people, and they less frequently consider ministries that stress discipleship or relational growth. Sometimes they even appear to be unaware that chaplains are already at work inside the institutions or that God's Spirit is also present, even before the invaders arrive. Nor do they sometimes understand that institutional worship services and religious groups are populated primarily by men or women who have already accepted Christ as Savior—who don't need to demonstrate that again at any altar call—and that their attendance at services reflect their desire to grow and learn how to better live out their faith commitments.

As a chaplain, I usually had volunteers from several nearby churches on a waiting list to conduct worship services or lead Bible studies, but I had difficulty finding members from those same churches who were willing to do the more difficult and less visible tasks of mentoring inmates or helping with reintegrating releasees into the community. Chaplains must accept, as a legitimate part of their ministry, the role of educating the local church and reshaping or redirecting its ministry impulses into activities that include offenders, their families, victims of crime, and at-risk populations in general. Wherever they have opportunity, they should actively promote theological thinking that incorporates perspectives of grace, forgiveness, acceptance, and an understanding of redemptive communities.

If crime is a moral issue, then who is going to teach morality if not the Church? If moral character is contained within the spiritual dimension of one's being, and if spiritual growth is essential to living a crime-free, moral life, who will nurture that spirituality if not the Church? However, the Church must first realize that the antidote for crime is contained within the teachings of Scripture and restorative communities rather than the mandates of anti-crime legislation. Only then, can they undertake ministry to those who violated their communities, and when that effort bears fruit, accept those prodigals who return home having admitted their wrongs and arrive asking for help in reordering their lives. The correctional chaplain, who understands the dynamics of criminal behavior and the socio-religious processes that overcome such behavior, is uniquely positioned to both direct the Church to its role in reducing crime and to assist the Church in fulfilling that call.

Chaplains should be community advocates for community programs that are based on restorative justice principles. Victim-centered, restorative justice is a comprehensive approach to crime that focuses on restoring the relationships that are destroyed by crime, not just on punishing the offender. It is restorative in the sense that it attempts to repair the damages done, to make things right, and to restore victims and offenders to peaceful communities. Central to restorative justice is an understanding of the Hebrew word, *shalom*, which is usually translated as "peace," but which expresses a far more complete understanding of that idea. The word carries the notion of harmony, fulfillment, and wholeness. "It is the ideal state in which the community is to function. It is not simply the absence of crime or war; it is also the security, prosperity and blessing that result from corporate righteousness" (Van Ness 120). Crime destroys this peace and creates a breach that must be repaired. Justice, then, should be a process that restores the sense of shalom that existed prior to a crime. It is both relational and redemptive (Van Ness 121).

The criminal justice system sees crime as an offense against the State, rather than as a violation of another individual. Operating from this faulty and incomplete perspective of the reality of crime, that system is never able to restore the necessary shalom to communities. If crime is a violation against the state, then crime has been reduced to mere lawbreaking, which means that justice becomes nothing more than affixing guilt and inflicting punishment. The whole process takes place on a field of conflict—the courtroom—where rules and intentions take precedence over outcomes (Zehr 65–81). In this impersonal arena, where abstract principles of law drive the process of dispensing justice, "forgiveness and mercy are nearly impossible to achieve" (82).

Chaplains understand that establishing guilt and making an offender pay for his/her crime is only the first step toward resolving the injury the offender has caused to the victim. The chaplain should understand, too, that his or her work cannot be confined inside the walls of the jail or prison; a comprehensive strategy for responding to crime must include educating the community outside. To think otherwise is to destine much of the chaplain's work to failure.

Seasoned chaplains have a great deal to contribute to issues of community reconciliation if they accept the role of minister to the community as well as to the inhabitants of their correctional facility.

ASSISTING WITH INMATE FAMILY CONCERNS

Almost always, when someone is arrested, a family is traumatized. The jail chaplain is called upon to assist families suddenly deprived of one of their members and thrust into a state of crisis because of that fact. It is impractical, and probably inappropriate, for the chaplain to have personal contact with the family outside the institution. First, there is simply not enough time to handle all the pastoral concerns of families in addition to those of prisoners themselves. Second, conflicts of interest easily emerge when an official of the institution—in this case the chaplain—becomes involved with issues that have potential legal implications.

Jail chaplains can, however, offer counsel to the confused or fearful husband or wife who contacts them in the midst of crisis. The chaplain may need to remind the spouse to seek legal counsel; he or she may be able to talk through possible solutions to financial problems; the chaplain can advise the spouse how to inform children of their parent's arrest and how to deal with the responses of those children; a chaplain may be able to assist the family member(s) in the grieving process that often results from the incarceration of a family member; in certain extreme cases, the chaplain may be able to arrange a special visit with the incarcerated spouse.

But undoubtedly the most significant assistance any jail or prison-based chaplain can provide to families is linkage with social services agencies in the community, correctional ministry organizations, or local churches that are sensitive to justice-related causes. Financial help, child care resources, job referrals, and emergency provisions such as food, shelter, and clothing are family needs that may arise at any time during the incarceration process. The chaplain soon finds that these are topics of serious concern for a large portion of the inmate population. As I have emphasized earlier, the effective chaplain will not limit his or her ministry by refusing to connect with other agencies or ministry providers. One of the chaplain's most important tasks is the development and maintenance of a resource guide with up-to-date information on available assistance within the community.

Of course, the chaplain is often dealing with a family located many miles away from the correctional facility that houses the husband, wife, son, or daughter. In those cases, the best approach is for the chaplain to contact the pastor of a church in the community where the family lives and ask that pastor for assistance. (The chaplain shouldn't be surprised to receive a reluctant response and thus should therefore be prepared to make more than one contact.)

Many of the concerns raised by inmate families reflect the difficulty they have in maintaining healthy relationships during periods of lengthy incarceration of a spouse. The chaplain may, then, be called upon to offer pastoral counseling involving marital issues that have been driven by dynamics unique to the prison setting. Enforced separation because of incarceration creates enormous stress on families, and divorce rates are high. Most state correctional departments recognize the importance of family cohesiveness and attempt, whenever possible, to house inmates in institutions close to their primary family. Still, *Dear John* or *Dear Jane* letters arrive at the prison with some frequency, and the inability of the inmate to communicate directly with his or her spouse creates tremendous frustration. It is the institutional chaplain who is there to share the inmate's burden when reconciliation efforts fail.

There is also what we can refer to as the **Jody syndrome.** In prison slang, *Jody* is a term used for the man who moves in with the prisoner's wife while the husband is serving his sentence. Strange as it may seem to those outside the correctional arena, the prisoner often gives implicit, if not explicit consent to this arrangement. Both inmate and wife may recognize the situation as immoral, yet continue to accept it as a viable survival strategy—a tolerable way of overcoming the economic and emotional pressures brought on by forced separation. (While husbands may be unfaithful to wives who are incarcerated, the Jody syndrome appears to be restricted to wives of male inmates, probably because females are often less able to provide adequate financial resources for the family's needs when the primary breadwinner is confined.) Once again, chaplains may have the opportunity, and the challenge, to lovingly speak God's truth into the midst of these situations in a noncondemnatory manner that has potential to motivate a lifestyle change.

All family-related conflictive situations are difficult to control from inside a jail or prison. *Hard time* is usually defined by inmates as living each day inside the prison while carrying the stressors of painful family situations, but without the ability to control many of the specifics connected with such problems. In fact, some prisoners cope with this by cutting themselves off from the pain emotionally and psychologically. They simply disengage, and in a manner of speaking, die. On the other hand, many continue trying to manage every facet of family life from behind prison walls—seldom appropriately and often disastrously. Prisoners are often quite unaware of the full impact their incarceration is having on their family. Their expectations and even the demands they make of their family can be unrealistic and burdensome.

One of the scenarios prisoners play out in their minds as their release date nears has to do with the reunion with their families. In the mental script, the now ex-prisoner walks through the front door shouting, "Honey, I'm home!" and everyone lives happily ever after. Unfortunately, this is far from the reality of a great many situations. The husband or wife left behind when the spouse goes off to prison adjusts to that spouse's absence. They learn an assortment of survival skills, become independent, and may become less than fully enthusiastic about the return of their mate. Moreover, the spouse may have begun to deal with previously submerged feelings of anger and resentment toward their prisoner-spouse whose behavior has jeopardized their marriage, financial well-being, home, and family relationships. In any of these cases, when the offender reenters the scene, issues frequently surface that threaten the family bonds.

At best, even when the spouse at home is eager to be reunited with his or her mate and even if both are attempting to walk with Christ, major readjustments are required. Prisoners tend to live in a mental vacuum, in a state of suspended animation where the world stops turning during the duration of their sentence. They often believe they can maintain relationships at the same level as the past, even though they now reside behind bars. They think they can resume those relationships at home as if they had never left, or as if their partner had also been vacuum sealed. These are the sorts of things the chaplain must consider as he or she thinks strategically about the worship opportunities, the teaching component, and the special programs needed to address such attitudes and actions at a spiritual level.

Thus far, I have been discussing reactive strategies for ministering to family needs; there are also proactive steps that chaplains can take to ease the strain on families forced to endure the imprisonment of one of their family members. These steps once again place the chaplain as an advocate within the Christian community, for they involve convincing that community to provide certain ministry services. First, in instances where a prisoner is housed a great distance from his or her family, transportation to the prison on visiting days is often a problem. If a car is available, it is not always reliable, nor is there always money for gas. In several locations around the country, chaplains have assisted churches in developing compassionate ministries to families by providing transportation for them to and from various prisons within their state.

In many cases, families can visit on consecutive days, but that creates the necessity of overnight accommodations, an economic barrier for many of them. Chaplains can encourage churches to consider providing a hospitality apartment to meet this need. As with the transportation ministry, this act of love provides an opportunity for mature Christians to develop relationships with family members that can lead to further opportunities to share about God, to disciple a struggling believer, or to offer spiritual insights into a myriad of life problems.

Another approach to family ministry involves establishing support groups for spouses or even children of prisoners. The church building or the home of a church member can provide the setting, and the group creates an unthreatening environment where families can share their common struggles and develop relationships with healthy faith-based facilitators. Here, too, the chaplain can provide insights that prepare laypersons to lead such groups.

There are many other possibilities for chaplains to link with community resources directed at the needs of families experiencing incarceration. For instance, marriage enrichment programs, conducted by parachurch prison and jail ministries and coordinated by the institutional chaplain, have proven effective in transmitting the spiritual strength to overcome problems and solidify the marriage bonds. Project Angel Tree, the Fatherhood Initiative, Child Evangelism, and other organizations have programs specifically designed to touch families and children of offenders or to work with the prisoner to develop or enhance their parenting skills. The success of these programs will be enhanced by a chaplain who is willing to expend extra effort to work them into the overall menu of services that flow from his or her office. In every case, chaplains are the pivotal persons whose contribution influences whatever degree of impact they may have.

ASSISTING WITH REENTRY OF OFFENDERS INTO THE COMMUNITY

The second most stressful time in a prisoner's incarceration (initial admission to jail ranks first) is that period immediately prior to release. From the perspective of the spike theory I introduced earlier, this stressful period provides a natural bridge for communication between the inmate and the chaplain. It also offers another example of how a chaplain's in-facility ministry is inextricably merged with community concerns. Although prisoners talk a lot about release, many times that talk is vague and unfocused. They may envision all sorts of romantic scenarios of what will take place, and they often approach the days of release with bravado and blind belief that they will "make it." In many cases, however, they fail to fully analyze the concrete problems that lie ahead. Thus, one of the chaplain's primary tasks is to motivate the inmate to do just that.

While in most institutions, the inmate's case manager is the primary point person for developing the post-release plan, the chaplain should make every effort to be included as an advisory voice, and when permitted, an active assistant in the process. Aside from that, the chaplain can have a great deal of informal influence by probing into areas of the inmate's plans that reach beyond the job and housing prospects—items that are the most concern to post-release supervising authorities. Good discussions starters might be: "Have you thought about what kind of mental and emotional adjustments you and your family are going to undergo when you come home to live?" or "How do you think your children are going to react to your first attempts to discipline them after having been away for so long?" These sorts of questions will prod the inmate's thinking and open the door for discussions about interpersonal and spiritual issues that are so critical to the ex-offender's successful reentry.

Sometimes, chaplains merely take an ineffective stab at pre-release counseling. They call the departing inmate into their office, ask a few perfunctory questions about future plans, and close the discussion with some attempt to inject faith issues into the framework of the inmate's future plans and offer a prayer of blessing. This may be better than no approach at all, but not by much. Chaplains can also play an integral part in a structured pre-release program where small to moderate-sized groups of future releasees meet over several weeks to discuss mutual concerns about life outside prison. If the institutional case management team does not provide such a program, then the chaplain should initiate and facilitate one with their blessing and input.

An effective pre-release program will confront inmates with key issues that will influence their potential to live productive lives in the free-world community. Probation and parole officers identify certain *criminogenic factors* they know to be crucial barriers to leading crime-free lives and that are clearly correlated with recidivism rates. These include such things as past criminal history, pro-criminal associates, educational achievement, and substance abuse. Supervisors of offenders who have been conditionally released to the community also emphasize the importance of employment and an appropriate residential setting. All of these are relatively easy to monitor—employers can be called, residences visited, and drug tests administered. But experts in this field also identify two other factors not easily monitored—appropriate thinking patterns and supportive family environments. These are precisely the arenas in which the chaplain can add great value. A pre-release program that addresses these areas, anticipating some of the difficulties the inmate will encounter and helping that man or woman formulate goal-oriented behaviors to manage the adjustment process can play a crucial role in determining whether or not the offender successfully navigates the difficult transition from prison to home.

Of course, some inmates *max out* their sentences and are released without supervision, many times with nowhere to go and no one to receive them. In these cases, the chaplain's task may be somewhat different. Most correctional systems provide a small check—$25 to $100—and a bus ticket that together are intended to supply the immediate needs of the releasee. However, if the ex-offender has no caring family to receive him or her, the ticket usually carries them back to the last place they called home, which is probably also the place where they encountered trouble with the law and where their former associates are poised to welcome them. The money runs out quickly, and the offender often reverts to a survival mode that quickly reengages him or her in a criminal lifestyle.

Chaplains can help the prisoner anticipate these situations and offer counsel on how best to avoid them. Most importantly, the chaplain can assist the inmate in contacting a church or faith-based correctional ministry in the receiving community and attempt to identify someone who will meet the ex-prisoner and help with the transition process. The potential for success may well be directly proportional to the depth of discussions the chaplain has had with the prisoner in the weeks prior to release in an effort to channel the inmate's thinking about life after prison into constructive paths. Still, much of that success is dependent on linkages the chaplain has maintained with the Christian community outside the institution.

But imprisonment changes people, usually for the worst. Donald Smarto speaks about the emotional and psychological damages prison inflicts and how this affects their ability to adjust to life outside the institution:

> I would liken this damage to the posttraumatic stress syndrome often observed in Vietnam veterans. These men and women experienced severe trauma as soldiers. When they came home, in order to function, they pushed the memories, thoughts, sights, and emotions deep inside—even into their subconscious minds. Eventually they became aware of both the experiences and of their defense mechanisms. But they continued to carry the bad memories as weighty baggage that hindered their ability to adjust to normal life. (Smarto 13)

People with serious behavioral problems are sentenced to prison. There, they are forced to live in a constricted environment with a large group of other people who have similar problem behaviors. Then, after being subjected to the peculiar sociopathies of a dangerous and demeaning institutional environment, they are released back into the community that formerly declared them unfit. Will these men and women reenter that world better prepared to live at peace with their fellow citizens? The skilled and informed chaplain can play a major role in determining that issue; he or she will be instrumental in any successful post-release experience.

Increasingly, correctional officials have begun to look to the community for assistance with a wide variety of program services. The reasons have become painfully obvious: Institutional programs alone, created and delivered primarily by correctional professionals from within the confines of the facility, have failed to produce significant measurable changes in offender behaviors.

Chaplains are limited in their ability to resolve many of the physical difficulties accompanying family problems or post-release issues. However, understanding the roles these issues play in the lives of those affected by incarceration enables the chaplain to better minister God's peace to those involved. Chaplains can also provide linkage to resources outside the institution, which are able to offer concrete assistance. Having personal limitations doesn't mean there are no solutions; it means that solutions may have to be found in the hands of others located outside the institution.

Increasingly, correctional officials have begun to look to the community for assistance with a wide variety of program services. The reasons have become painfully obvious: Institutional programs alone, created and delivered primarily by correctional professionals from within the confines of the facility, have failed to produce significant measurable changes in offender behaviors. The faith factor, so long ignored, has in recent years been recognized as a potentially important element of correctional treatment strategies. This significant shift in correctional philosophy should signal a need for chaplains to revise their thinking as well, and to recognize that an important dimension of their ministry encompasses meaningful engagement with the community outside the institution and the systems that operate it.

Recently, some states have begun to follow an idea originating this past decade in Canada—the notion of establishing community-based chaplains whose role it is to aid returning offenders in the reentry process. Oregon, Colorado, and more recently Texas are examples. Although this trend may continue, in an era of dwindling governmental resources, it is doubtful that much of this will be publically funded. What is more realistic to assume is that the institutional chaplain will be called upon to play a lead role in identifying and collaborating with faith-based institutions and community agencies to create effective reentry roadmaps. This role is not only a natural fit for the chaplain who operates by the principles expressed in this chapter, but as I have tried to demonstrate, it is a role that merges the ministry behind the walls with that of the larger Church within the community. This union will expand and revitalize the notions of correctional chaplaincy and that the community dimension will become the launching point for the next significant evolution within the profession.

REFERENCES

Van Ness, Daniel W. (1996). *Crime and its Victims: What We Can Do*. Downers Grove, IL: InterVarsity Press.

Smarto, Donald. (1994). *Keeping Ex-Offenders Free! An Aftercare Guide*. Grand Rapids, MI: Baker Books.

Zehr, Howard. (1990). *Changing Lenses*. Scottdale, PA: Herald Press.

Chapter Nine

The Individualized Ministry Plan

We have proposed that the work of the correctional chaplain has three critical dimensions that can be viewed as a structural frame from which chaplaincy always flows, regardless of the individual setting in which it takes place. Now it is time to address some practical matters regarding the realities of the ministry as it functions in specific settings. While it is essential to keep the big picture in mind at all times—the framework—the on-the-ground work of chaplains unfolds within specific facilities whose missions may vary considerably from one to another and may change at some given point. In any case, the chaplain can overlay this three-dimensional template of chaplaincy on any institution as a way of maintaining quality control in a constantly evolving professional environment. Using it as a lens through which he or she views the overall mission, the chaplain can then develop a strategic ministry plan that is responsive to the individual properties of any distinct facility.

> *The process of building an individualized ministry plan begins with a careful analysis of the physical and operational design of the jail or prison and the demographics of the inmate population housed within its perimeter.*

The process of building an individualized ministry plan begins with a careful analysis of the physical and operational design of the jail or prison and the demographics of the inmate population housed within its perimeter. The questions we will consider in this chapter highlight most of the critical variables that exist within any institution and that might influence the programs and services a chaplain is called upon to deliver. Chaplains should respond to each of them by gathering accurate information, not just estimations, and then factor that information into the planning of an institutional-specific ministry plan. For our purposes here, I will offer comments after each question as a way of pointing out the potential significance of each item and as a guide to the nature of the considerations each chaplain should make.

To the newly assigned chaplain, or to one who is considering this ministry, this will be quite informative; however, more experienced chaplains may initially feel as if they already have a firm grasp on the dynamics of their institutions. That is partly because they have absorbed these things over time through a process of osmosis. But even in my work with experienced chaplains, I have been surprised at how many of them know the basic facts about their facility and understand the underlying concepts discussed here, yet still fail to align the components of their program offerings with what the information suggests. In short, they don't think strategically, and as a result, are considerably less effective than they might be. Beyond that, there is the ongoing challenge all of us face in maintaining freshness in those things we do with regularity. Even seasoned chaplains need to discipline themselves to go through an annual review and planning cycle, and these questions will contribute to that. The proactive process I present here is one way of enhancing the planning process, avoiding many false starts, and keeping the chaplain's mission fully aligned with the work environment.

DEMOGRAPHIC ANALYSIS

Jail: Does the institution have a mission statement? What is it?

The fact that jails primarily serve local communities means they vary a great deal in size, resources, and sophistication of operation. While all jails are classified as temporary holding facilities, they may have more specific agendas attached to their mission. Some federal detention facilities, for instance, may serve specific populations, e.g., ICE detainees. Regional jails are characterized by their commitment to multicounty jurisdictions, a fact that may alter their ultimate operational processes to some degree. Some metropolitan jails act as initial receiving centers from which inmates are quickly transported to nearby county jails. The nature of the written mission statement, then, will also vary; some smaller county institutions may make simple, straightforward, and generalized claims, while larger urban jails have lengthier and more encompassing statements. In any event, digesting the mission statement is the first step in thinking through what chaplaincy services should look like at that location.

Prison: Does the institution have a mission statement apart from the general mission of the Department of Corrections or Bureau of Prisons? If so, what do both say?
Any prison that is a part of a larger system, whether state or federal, will share a common mission; however, the particular unit itself may have a specific purpose that is subservient to the more general statement. The federal system categorizes its institutions by mission and names them accordingly—either on the basis of their security or the specialized populations they hold. Thus, Federal Prison Camps (FPCs) are minimum security units; Federal Correctional Institutions (FCIs) hold low security or medium inmates; and United States Penitentiaries (USPs) house primarily high security prisoners. Other centers holding certain special populations have unique names, as well. Unlike the federal system, state departments of corrections are not as likely to distinguish missions through their official designation. They may also vary as to the degree of clear differentiation of mission and are prone to having multiple specialized units within individual facilities. For instance, more than one prison in a system might have medical units or special management blocks, though there is a trend toward segregated administrative-maximum facilities that house extremely dangerous or violent individuals.

The point in carefully considering the institutional mission statement—whether that is a jail, a prison, or a specialized facility—is for the chaplain to pinpoint where the delivery of chaplaincy services falls within the overall goals and purposes of that facility. What is there in the mission that validates the ministry of the chaplain? Where does the chaplain see him or herself fitting into the overall staffing plan? What specific programs are called for that both serve the religious needs of the inmate population and are also fully compatible with the goals of the correctional setting?

By way of example, the Florida Department of Correction's current mission statement is: *To protect the public safety, to ensure the safety of Department personnel, and to provide proper care and supervision of all offenders under our jurisdiction while assisting, as appropriate, their re-entry into society.* One can easily recognize a clear match with the critical dimensions of chaplaincy in two areas: proper care of offenders (pastoral dimension) and assisting with their preparation to reenter society (pastoral and community dimensions). Somewhere within the context of any DOC mission statement, there will be a defined territory where chaplaincy can be placed and from which it can successfully launch its fully orbed ministry. Understanding this precise point of occupancy is important when interfacing with administrators whom you want to always understand why you do what you do, and why specific programs are designed as they are. If you are unable to justify your programs on the basis of institutional concerns, they will be in serious jeopardy, as they should be!

This is a good place to identify a crucial distinction between jails and prisons. Jails are much like hospital emergency rooms: They are trauma centers where wounds abound, blood flows freely, and people wait in pain to see just how serious their injuries are and what treatment will be administered. Friends and family stand by in the waiting room, sharing the pain and the uncertain future of their loved ones. Jail chaplains attend to the most crucial immediate needs: stopping the flow of blood, minimizing the pain, and offering reassurance to family members. The majority of the jail chaplain's time is spent in counseling with inmates about immediate needs, offering comfort and hope during a time of great stress, interacting with social agencies or directly with families to initiate needed assistance, and distributing religious literature.

As facilities for temporary or short-term detention, jails are not designed for programs. Space is usually at a premium—as is security staff—so movement of the inmate population is kept to a minimum, and as a result, no chapel or other activity areas may be available for worship services, Bible studies, or any special service. Often, jail chaplains deliver sermons from corridors outside cell blocks or in open spaces inside housing pods. Correspondence courses may substitute for Bible study, and the number of volunteer-led programs is minimal. In keeping with our medical metaphor, we might say that the jail chaplain's role is to help stabilize the "patient" by attending to immediate needs before that person is moved to a more permanent location (a prison) where a long-term therapeutic strategy is employed (by a prison chaplain).

Prisons usually have considerable program space, and except for highly specialized facilities that house exceptional offenders, their mission calls for strategic intervention efforts by the program staff. Chaplains in these locations, then, operate with rehabilitative and reformative agendas that can be implemented over time and evaluated accordingly. The family dynamics are different and often begin to deteriorate as time passes.

On the other hand, the extended sentence length allows for growth-oriented religious education programs, multiple counseling sessions that provide chaplains time to probe more deeply into the inmate deficits, and inmates have a full range of chapel services and special religious events in which they may participate. If the jail is the ER, then prison is the hospital. This model suggests that evangelism efforts may bear more fruit in local jails, when anxiety levels are highest, than in the prison setting after the immediate crisis has passed and some acceptance of the conditions has taken place. In contrast, religious programs within prisons offer opportunities for long-term discipleship and monitored values clarification and adjustment.

What is the average daily population of the institution, and what is its ethnic and religious distribution?

ACA Standards call for one full-time staff chaplain to be assigned to any institution with an average daily population of 500 or more inmates (*ACA Standard 4–4513*). The intent seems to be to establish a 1-to-500 ratio as an acceptable span of control for each staff chaplain. Thus, a facility with 1,000 inmates should have two chaplains, and so on. However, I'm not sure any institution in the country fully staffs at that ratio; as long as there is one full-time chaplain assigned, the institution is technically in compliance. At the same time, there is no well-supported argument for why this is a magical ratio. Nonetheless, size is certainly one critical variable in how a chaplain structures a ministry plan and prioritizes various items contained within it. There is some finite work load that is manageable, though that varies from chaplain to chaplain; and as a general rule job stress will increase with more administrative traffic flow. However, my observation is that the number of inmates housed has less impact on staffing requirements than the specialized nature of that population and the physical characteristics of the prison design.

If the institution has 1,000 inmates that are accurately classified as *general population*, it is understaffed with only one chaplain. If, on the other hand, those 1,000 inmates are in *administrative segregation*, one chaplain has a far better chance of adequately meeting their needs because of their restricted mobility and the limited number of appropriate programs that can be delivered. There are also facilities that, by the nature of their physical design, need extra staffing regardless of the number of people they house. Sometimes this is because they were built for one use and their mission was later changed; at other times, a facility was originally used for some non-correctional purpose and then retrofitted as a prison; and in some cases, additional sections were constructed over time to house specialized classifications, and the facility evolved into a series of separate structures almost indiscriminately pasted together. In any event, the size of the population shouldn't be an arbitrary factor in determining staffing needs.

In considering both programs and staffing needs, the chaplain must also take into consideration the percentages of various ethnicities and religions that are distributed across the facility population to ensure that there is an adequate representation of each in the total program mix. On one occasion when I was reviewing a chaplain's ministry plan, I asked the chaplain about the ethnic distribution in his institution. When he provided the data, I pointed to the 30 percent of his population that was of Hispanic origin and asked him what programs he had in place for this segment of the population. He explained that a Spanish-speaking Catholic priest was periodically available for confession or celebrating Mass, but that there was nothing else offered. When I probed deeper, I found that there was reason to believe that a sizeable segment of this population was Protestant, but there was no program offering dedicated to them, either. "Do you think your chaplaincy programs are fairly representative of your population?" I asked.

He agreed that, when I put it that way, perhaps it wasn't. Even though he was not quite sure where to begin to rectify the situation, he committed to making that effort. Within a month he had managed to locate a Catholic deacon who agreed to lead a weekly group study, and a few days after that, the chaplain phoned to tell me that a conversation with one of the Hispanic correctional officers had led to scheduling a monthly worship service for those believers. Thinking strategically helped this chaplain understand some limitations in his program plan and to resolve it in a way that blessed everyone and extended the reach of the pastoral dimension of his ministry.

What is the general security designation of the institution?

As a rule of thumb, the higher the security level, the more restricted is any inmate movement and the less opportunity allotted for programs from the chaplaincy department. If the inmates are not free to move between places to attend a worship service or group studies, the chaplain has to take those opportunities to their housing areas, as security demands permit. If those programs are volunteer-led, that may present new challenges—perhaps additional security clearances or monitoring procedures. Sometimes, though, the overall security designation reflects the highest allowable level of inmates housed, rather than the status of the majority. In that case, the restrictions may be confined to certain areas of the facility, which means the chaplain's planning must be multidimensional.

Counseling opportunities are also impacted by restrictions that grow out of security designations. If movement is curtailed, inmates can't simply drop by the chaplain's office for spontaneous conversations; they must have a pass, and perhaps even be escorted. In jails, of course, that is seldom an option. In high security locales, the chaplain may have to respond to a written request by personally visiting the inmate's housing unit—a time-consuming alternative. It is also less easy for the chaplain to visit those units, since each entrance creates an imposition of some degree for correctional officers. And there is the fact that prisoners are not always willing for other inmates to know they have scheduled a conversation with the chaplain. Information about one's struggles or personal situations can be a source of power for others to use to their advantage, so meetings with the chaplain are often veiled in secrecy. Those opportunities are seriously curtailed in higher security settings.

Of course, the opposite of all this holds true for minimal security institutions. Easy access, open movements, and the placement of more trust in the residents expand the opportunities for programs. This means that the chaplain has a new set of problems—managing multiple calendar options and supervising the volunteers that automatically accompany those activities. Lower security usually signifies that either the inmates have committed lesser offenses or that they are nearer the end of the sentences and have earned a reduction in their classification. In either case, the chaplain will need to consider program options that meet their specific criminogenic backgrounds and matches well with the proximity of their release date.

Is the facility structured to manage any special inmate population (age, nature of offense, mental health designation, etc.)? If so identify those special management units and note where they are located within the institution.

Special management units call for special planning on the part of the chaplain to ensure that the inmates involved in those units are incorporated into the overall ministry strategy. These groups will, by their very nature, receive more attention from other staff—from both the treatment and the security side. Their engagement with staff will be more intense and more frequent, and the staff will often have special training certifications. In some cases, these units are extremely high profile and may stand as signature programs for the broader prison system. Most of these will be driven by public safety or psycho-social concerns, with little or no thought given to the spiritual dimension of the inmate. That means chaplains can easily be left out of the equation and may be tempted to allow that to continue, to their detriment.

I strongly encourage chaplains to develop meaningful relationships with the teams that manage these sites, for several reasons. In the first place, none of the behaviors these units are designed to address—whether anger management, substance abuse, mental health, etc.—is bereft of a spiritual component, though the staff members who supervise these units may not easily accept that fact. Second, out of professional courtesy and institutional efficiency, it is essential for all the separate program divisions to interface effectively. It is especially important that chaplains and any other treatment team members communicate with each other, share mutually beneficial information, and coordinate their approaches to any inmate's needs. Chaplains should attempt to carve out an active role, when possible, and at the very least an advisory role in the program delivery of these units. But even if the chaplain is not included at a minimal staffing level, he or she still must incorporate the needs of this segment of the prison population into the ministry plan, and given the heavy involvement of the other programs, this will present some special challenges.

Other specialized settings would include those devoted to inmates with medical needs. Usually, every prison system has at least one facility dedicated to housing these individuals. Still, for various reasons, there may be some segment of this population maintained in facilities that have other primary missions. In configuring their ministry plan, chaplains need to determine how to work this special housing unit into the overall approach. Someone from the chaplaincy team needs to regularly visit the inmates there, and the problem of worship and religious study opportunities must be addressed. This population also has counseling needs that differ from the other institutional population, so the decision of which particular chaplain or seasoned volunteer responds to these men or women is an important one.

It many states, as well as in the Federal Bureau of Prisons, entire prisons are given over to administrative-maximum facilities that house extremely dangerous and violent offenders who are locked down in single cells for all but an hour each day. These individuals are not permitted to congregate with anyone, nor attend any program, and standard protocol is that even pastoral visits require the presence of at least two correctional officers and the inmate to be shackled. How in the world does the chaplain provide these prisoners any of the worship and study opportunities normally afforded inmates in other prisons? What strategies can the chaplain employ to provide them a way to exercise their constitutional rights to practice their religion?

That was the problem another of the chaplains I worked with once faced. We resolved the dilemma by getting permission to tap into the already existing closed circuit video system and supply a weekly on-demand worship service through an open channel. In addition, we devised a process for inmates to request a series of Bible studies available on DVD that could be initiated from a central point and be played over that same channel. Without creating any security hazards, and with just a small measure of extra administrative labor, we provided a vicarious worship experience and a legitimate study method for any inmate who sought spiritual direction. No one would have blamed the chaplain of that facility for accepting what appeared to be insurmountable limitations, but through careful analysis and proactive planning, we successfully fulfilled the pastoral dimension of chaplaincy in that facility.

Describe the characteristics of the housing units within the institution (dorms, pods, temporary units, etc.) and indicate the size of each.

This information is usefully primarily in those facilities where program and private meeting space is at a premium and requires that programs and/or personal counseling sessions take place inside housing units. Usually, this will be jail, although it may also be true of some small special population prison facilities. Worship and study opportunities are critical to one's faith, as is access to a spiritual counselor, so failing to offer these simply because the space isn't conducive to them isn't an option—the chaplain works with what he or she has and adjusts. Still, the situation does present unique problems. I have had occasion to engage in some pretty emotional counseling scenarios while sitting at picnic tables in the day rooms of jail pods—not a desirable situation, but there were no other options. In similar spaces, I have conducted rather subdued worship services that more closely resembled Bible studies in an effort to honor the privacy of other inmates sitting nearby. I have delivered death notifications inside the offices of correctional staff when there was no better option available. The chaplain needs to know everything about the peculiarities of the housing accommodations and factor them into the ministry plan from its inception.

Overcrowding is a serious problem within many jails and prisons. Apart from the legalities involved—about which chaplains can do little—the added dehumanization, danger, and potential health issues that arise from this situation increase tensions, adds stress, and fuels violence. Savvy chaplains will do whatever they can to alleviate the added pains of incarceration brought on by crowded housing arrangements. A calming ministry of presence is extremely important in these situations, as is addressing the emotional and behavioral stressors—however obliquely—in sermons and religious study sessions. These conditions certainly call for the chaplain to be more security-conscious and extra sensitive to the potential hazards faced by volunteers. In most cases, it will also impact the ministry plan, since programs will probably be limited to some degree.

What portion of the inmate population in the institution is required to work inside the facility? For how many hours each day and at what times? During a normal day, what percentage of the population is assigned to educational programs? How many hours and on which days?

Not infrequently, chaplains devise activity schedules that match their working schedule or that of the volunteer's preferences, instead of one that matches the needs of the inmate population. Particularly in minimum security institutions, but in any facility where a significant number of inmates spend a portion of their day working outside the perimeter, the chaplain must consider these routines in establishing times for program offerings. Usually, inmate work schedules call for half-day or alternative workday schedules in a predictable routine that allows them to engage with religious programs if the chaplain has carefully considered their responsibilities when planning the calendar. The same is true of any educational assignment, whether it is voluntary or mandated. Careful planning and sensitivity to this element of the population is important.

It is worth noting here, however, that sometimes the inmate may be better served by participating in an AA group, a program that addresses thinking errors, or any of a number of programs directed at some pertinent behavioral deficit. The chaplain should never claim some sort of superiority of religious programs; the goal is not to compete for the inmate's time, but simply to ensure adequate availability to everyone. This only occurs with careful planning and deliberate effort.

Is there a dedicated chapel within the facility, or do religious services use a multipurpose area? Are there additional rooms available for small group activities? Are these only used for religious programs? Describe any area available for individual counseling.

The final physical assessment must be directed at analyzing the available space and determining how that space can be utilized. In institutions that have a dedicated space for religious activities, scheduling is less complex, since there are usually no nonreligious activities competing for available space. I say "usually" because in some smaller facilities, what has been designated as a chapel might be the only space for any sizeable group assembly, and therefore the chaplain may be asked to share space with recreational activities or other secular programs. I encountered this in one institution where I served as chaplain, and although I was willing to work with other departments, I did find myself in a lively discussion with the warden over the nature of the films being shown in the sacred space of our chapel (I won some concessions). If the space is strictly reserved for religious programs, the problem is a different one—now the chaplain must carefully allocate space for all recognized religions without partiality. That does not mean that each religious group gets an equal amount of time, but it does argue for access to all and for proportional scheduling.

Hopefully, there is also adequate space for small group activities, though that is seldom available for the exclusive use of the chaplaincy. Likewise, smaller rooms or offices are desirable for those individual counseling sessions that require a measure of privacy. Chaplains will have to work with what they have, but they need to know precisely what that is and what the parameters of usage are to adequately create the facility ministry plan.

STAFFING ANALYSIS

Once the chaplain has a clear picture of the physical characteristics of the institution itself and certain key demographics of the inmate population, he or she needs to examine the staffing resources available. There's no use designing what can't be appropriately staffed, and building an idealistic model that will quickly be subjected to realistic shortcomings is an exercise in futility and frustration. The chaplain begins with an understanding that the three critical dimensions must be managed and then, after surveying the physical factors that are largely fixed and unchangeable, considers what human resources are available and what boundaries they are subject to that could impact their delivery of ministry services.

How many full-time chaplains serve in the facility? How many part-time chaplains?

First, the chaplain needs to determine how many total hours are available for service delivery. If, as is often the case, the chaplain is the only full-time staff member and is dependent on part-time assistance, the available work times of the part-timer will seldom be negotiable. The chaplain will probably be the one whose schedule demands flexibility. The part-time chaplain is often a well-trained and experienced volunteer who, though quite capable, may not have full access to all facility space—another planning consideration.

Are there any inmate clerks assigned to the chaplain? How many and how many hours are they available? Are there institutional staff members who provide administrative support?

Chapter Seven discussed the administrative dimension in depth, and the salient point was made that fulfilling these tasks should be seen as legitimate ministry. In creating the facility plan, then, the chaplain needs to understand exactly what administrative items can be picked up by adjunct members of the team, either inmate clerks or other correctional staff members who have been tasked with supporting this area. Inmate clerical support can be invaluable, even though security concerns will place limits on what sort of information they can access.

Sometimes, too, the assignment of clerks appears to be made more on the basis of having a heart for the position than on whether or not that inmate possesses competent skills that match the chaplain's actual needs. Any staff member assigned to the chaplain will most likely support other personnel, as well, so the need often outstrips the available internal resources. This is a place where volunteers can also prove to be invaluable assets. All in all, chaplains will have ample opportunity to practice their managerial skills in this area.

Although any chaplain's supervisor may rightfully question additional programs that change space allocations, influence correctional staffing patterns, create added security demands, or that stretch traditional definitions of religious activities, those supervisors should not make decisions about program validity or act as censors of what they believe to be appropriate.

What is the approval process for initiating a new program?

This question has to do with the autonomy of the chaplain. Throughout this text, we have directed our discussion to that professional chaplain occupying the position of program head with authority to oversee this area of expertise and the freedom to develop it accordingly, subject to normal facility authority structures. Sometimes the reality is considerably different.

In cases where the chaplaincy role has been given less respect than it deserves, the chaplain may have a supervisor who has co-opted the role of content expert and evaluator—a job that should remain under the purview of the chaplain alone. Although any chaplain's supervisor may rightfully question additional programs that change space allocations, influence correctional staffing patterns, create added security demands, or that stretch traditional definitions of religious activities, those supervisors should not make decisions about program validity or act as censors of what they believe to be appropriate. That is the chaplain's job, and unless he or she has proven to be incapable or untrustworthy, that role should not be invalidated, but we have seen recent encroachment in this area.

While supervisors should be free to discuss anything they feel is questionable, at the end of the conversation, the supervisor should trust the wisdom of the expert on matters of faith. Hopefully, the chaplain consistently rewards that trust. Whatever the approval process is, the chaplain needs to be absolutely sure he or she knows what it is and honors it. With full understanding of that process, the chaplain can then carefully construct any documentation that is required and realistically calculate the turnaround time for initiating any new program venture. Over time, some programs will need to be adjusted or eliminated, and new offers established. Becoming agile at this process is an essential chaplaincy skill.

Does the chaplain supervise (approve, schedule, and monitor) all religious programs or only that of his/her faith tradition?

Increasingly, as we have pointed out in an earlier section of this book, chaplains are being steered toward administrative roles and most often coordinate all religious activities as a part of their duties. At the same time, another dynamic at work is that the institutional staff members are more frequently being assigned this role, irrespective of the absence of any theological training or pastoral experience in their background. Perhaps it is a high-ranking officer who oversees the programs division, or it may be the volunteer services coordinator. In that environment, there are many occasions where the designated chaplain serves only his or her faith, with the institutional administrator bearing the responsibility for overseeing multiple faith group providers. This is an undesirable situation, but an unfortunate reality in some jurisdictions and the chaplain may have to adjust accordingly.

In what specific ways does the chaplain interact with faith-group volunteers?

An earlier chapter discussed this topic at length, and we stressed the responsibility as well as the satisfactions of recruiting, training, and assessing volunteers to faithfully deliver critical services. In some jails or prisons, the chaplain will have the ability to do all of those things. In others, a staff member may be assigned to the orientation and training of all volunteers, which leaves only the specific instructions about program content to be handled by the chaplain. Still, the job of recruiting faith-based volunteers will probably always fall to the chaplain.

One essential piece must be determined: Who is responsible to see that all necessary paperwork is completed, and who is responsible for security clearances? One thing is always a clear priority—careful processing to ensure quality control of those who represent your office in any engagement with both inmates and correctional staff. Too often, chaplains function as if the desire of a volunteer is equivalent to the possession of adequate skills, or as if verbal acknowledgements equate to tested behaviors. Chaplains should never shortcut the careful investigation of volunteer backgrounds and should always insist on personally contacting references of anyone being considered for a ministry role in the jail or prison. There are few things more damaging to the chaplain's credibility or more stifling to new program development than a volunteer who violates established rules.

To whom does the chaplain directly report within the facility? Is the chaplain required to provide any periodic written reports to the institutional supervisor? In place of, or in addition to a written report, is there a regularly scheduled time for reporting verbally, as well?

In days past, when religion had more currency within the justice system, prison chaplains often reported directly to the deputy warden in charge of care and treatment programs—or even to the warden—and it was not unusual for the jail chaplain to have direct access to the sheriff. Today, chaplains usually find themselves farther down the food chain. Jail chaplains may be positioned directly below the jail commander, but in larger facilities may find themselves at least one step removed from that. Prison chaplains in these times almost always report to a programs manager—either line staff or a civilian employee—who in turn may report to a deputy within the facility, but who also interfaces with an administrator located in the central office of the department of corrections. These layers can present murky waters for the chaplain who is trying to administrate a wide-ranging menu of chaplaincy services. It is easy to become confused about who has authority over certain segments of the total effort, and the chaplain has to have clarity on these matters.

Careful documentation of everything is crucial, as is open dialogue with those who directly oversee the chaplain's efforts. This is also where the chaplain's ongoing building of relationships becomes most important. The chaplain who has even an occasional audience with the superintendent/ warden or sheriff has a distinct advantage whenever he or she is called upon to defend a program or process, or is attempting to introduce new initiatives.

Similarly, the chaplain who communicates both well and frequently has far more potential for success with any aspect of the operational ministry plan. Regardless of what is formally required by way of reporting, I encourage chaplains to regularly provide written reports about departmental goals, successes, and new initiatives to immediate supervisors, and unless expressly forbidden, to copy other parties linked in the immediate chain of accountability.

Is the chaplain asked to monitor any nonreligious activities?

This is introduced as a cautionary point. One of the trends that has surfaced as a direct result of the erosion of the pastoral dimension of chaplaincy is the use of chaplains for tasks unrelated to religious activities. This is a slippery slope that every chaplain needs to resist. Logic has it that administrators administrate. So the argument goes, if chaplains are viewed primarily as program administrators rather than as pastors, why shouldn't they be asked to oversee other nonreligious activities? My answer is that the *office* of *pastor* precludes this. Would correctional officers be asked to preach or teach a Bible study, even if they might possess adequate knowledge to do so at a minimal level? They would not, because that is not their assigned institutional role—they are security personnel, and are tasked accordingly. So, too, chaplains should resist any request to regularly perform duties that are outside their assigned role as religious leader. This is why it is crucial that the pastoral dimension of chaplaincy must always remain central to the position description, and why chaplains must continue to jealously guard this divinely ordained role.

THE INSTITUTIONAL MINISTRY PLAN

Having analyzed the institutional demographics and calculated the extent of the staffing resources available, the chaplain is prepared to create the facility ministry plan. This is really a two-phase design. One part of it should reflect the schedule of institutional activities and routines of the chaplaincy team, but a second—and more important—component is a goal-oriented performance plan that can be reviewed annually and that serves as a self-imposed assessment tool. On the basis of the information gathered, the chaplain will determine:

- The appropriate institutional work schedule for each member of the team.
- The number of worship services and study groups allocated for all faith groups, along with their scheduled meeting times and the location of each.
- Who delivers and/or monitors each activity.
- Tentative calendar slots reserved for special nonrecurring program events.
- The necessary reporting mechanism in place for both institutional accountability and chaplaincy services.

As the scheduling plan develops, the chaplain will have to decide how many, if any, activities he or she personally leads. Most chaplains will probably want to handle some of these, but the number will depend on the size of the institution and the complexity of ministry services, as well as how the chaplain feels about his or her particular giftings.

The chaplain should also create a personal schedule of work activities that encompasses the other critical routines of service:

- Visiting selected locations within the institution as a part of an overall ministry of presence.
- Visiting restricted populations to identify needs and/or fulfill inmate requests for service.
- Periodic appearance at shift changes and regularly scheduled meetings with supervisors.
- Office time designated for counseling appointments, or if the institution accommodates times of free movement, for drop-in visits by either inmates or staff.
- Office time set aside for planning and completing essential paperwork.

This is also the point at which the chaplain identifies specific legitimate opportunities to interact with community agencies and solicits an agreement with the facility's administration to allocate some time off the institutional grounds.

The schedule will never unfold exactly as planned—there will always be intrusions—but that is no excuse to fail to plan. Every chaplain I have observed who has a systematic approach to their daily and weekly routine gets more accomplished and is far more effective than the ones who simply show up each day and rely on spontaneous responses to whatever arises. After all, if you don't know where you're going, any road will take you there; if you do know where you're going, then you'll always find the best way to get there. To repeat a point made earlier—the degree to which a chaplain effectively administrates his or her delivery of ministry services is the degree to which that chaplain will have maximum impact.

Ministry Plan Assessment

When it comes to assessing the institutional impact of chaplaincy services, most professionals point to quantitative measurements—how many programs delivered, hours invested, inmates participating, volunteers involved, and estimated lawsuits avoided. Of course chaplains are subject to performance reviews, but these have little to do with the effectiveness of the programs they manage apart from those numbers described. Seldom has there been any effort to develop an outcomes-based evaluation of ministry delivery. Here, an important distinction should be made, one that most professions clearly embrace. *Output* is simply a measure of activity—the amount of energy expended. *Outcome,* however, describes results achieved—a measure of effectiveness. Applying that principle, I believe we have been measuring the wrong things, and the health of our profession demands a better approach. The second phase of the individualized ministry plan I propose provides a beginning point for an outcomes-based approach to evaluating performance.

Using the subtopics contained within each of the four *critical dimensions* discussed in chapters five through eight, the chaplain should then develop objectives for each category and fashion a written ministry plan that is consistent with the objectives of his or her specific facility. That document can then be reviewed annually to evaluate accomplishments and identify areas where objectives need to be adjusted or ministry delivery reconfigured. Here is the plan schematic.

CRITICAL DIMENSIONS OF CHAPLAINCY

Personal Development
- Maintaining a Healthy Spiritual Relationship
- Maintaining Effective Personal Relationships
- Sustaining an Active Agenda for Professional Development

Pastoral Ministry
- Sharing the Good News of God's love
- Offering Supportive Counseling
- Leading Worship, Providing Religious Instruction, and Promoting Spiritual Growth
- Maintaining a Ministry of Presence within the Facility
- Building Relationships with Staff

Administrative
- Developing and Maintaining an Institutional Ministry Plan
- Developing Volunteers: Recruiting, Training, Supervising/Assessing
- Interfacing with Ministry Organization Leadership
- Interfacing with Institutional Leadership
- Facilitating all Recognized Faith Groups

Community
- Fostering Community Awareness and Partnerships
- Educating the Church and Community about Justice Ministries
- Assisting with Inmate Family Concerns
- Assisting with Reentry of Offenders into the Community

I recommend using the SMART formula for setting objectives. SMART objectives are:

Specific
Measureable
Achievable
Realistic
Time-bound

So, for example, one objective for the coming year that falls under the third component of the *pastoral dimension* might be stated like this:

Leading Worship, Providing Religious Instruction, and Promoting Spiritual Growth

Objective: To emphasize that Scriptural principles have direct application to day-to-day life situations.

1. *I will personally lead one worship service each month.*
2. *I will personally lead two Bible Studies each week.*
3. *I will create a one-page study guide each week and make it available for any interested inmates upon request.*

Similarly, an objective with corresponding action statements for bullet two of the administrative dimension might read as follows:

Developing Volunteers: Recruiting, Training, Supervising/Assessing

Objective: To expand and enhance the current volunteer base.

1. *I will recruit and gain approval of 12 volunteers over the course of the year.*
2. *I will conduct quarterly training sessions for all volunteers who lead any program.*

3. *I will visit each volunteer-supervised activity once every six months and provide written feedback to the volunteer leader.*

While the chaplain should consider every item on the Critical Dimensions of Chaplaincy document and identify at least one objective for each, this is not to say that every item, or even every category within each dimension, is of equal importance at any given moment in history. That is not the case. For instance, a chaplain might be newly assigned to an institution where many program components are established and appear to be functioning well; in that case the first year objectives would probably center on evaluation and maintenance, as opposed to new program development. Or the opposite might be true—the chaplain opens a new facility where nothing is in place, in which year one is entirely devoted to establishing baseline services. In established chaplaincies, some objectives might be directed at repairing something that has clearly become broken or some might need attention only because of staffing disruptions. Each year, some elements will shift, and as they do, new priorities are established and objectives changed. Perhaps the mission of the institution changes, which calls for a serious review and potential revamping of nearly every ministry offering.

The point is that although individual program offerings or staffing routines change as a result of new realities, the template doesn't change. We have defined the *critical dimensions of chaplaincy,* and in so doing, have developed both an enduring identity and established broad parameters of the mission. However, the individualized ministry plan enables that mission to be carried out in ways that meet the distinctives of any correctional setting, and it provides a document that can be reviewed to monitor results and revised accordingly.

> *The individualized ministry plan is a tool that helps chaplains formulate facility-specific goals based on clear objectives derived from the critical dimensions of their profession; assess their performance on the basis of measurable outcomes; and reformulate their ministry strategies accordingly.*

In one of Charles Shultz's classic cartoons, Charlie Brown is at camp taking part in an archery class. When one of the other characters comments on Charlie's amazing ability to hit bull's-eyes, Charlie says, "Well, I do it a bit differently. I first shoot the arrow, and then I go and draw a bull's-eye around where it hits." The fact is that we can appear to be effective at anything we do if we mark the target after we've completed the tasks. The individualized ministry plan is a tool that helps chaplains formulate facility-specific goals based on clear objectives derived from the critical dimensions of their profession; assess their performance on the basis of measurable outcomes; and reformulate their ministry strategies accordingly. With regular use, it should also sharpen their ability to deliver quality performance.

Chapter Ten

Back to the Future

Correctional chaplaincy has evolved from a voluntary effort led by interested community pastors into a complex, specialized profession—one that is both demanding and rewarding. As we have seen, it is also a profession that continues to change and redefine itself in light of current demands. In this text, we have briefly reviewed the history of the profession, charted some of those role adjustments, and proposed a set of the foundational principles upon which this ministry rests. Then, we presented a structural paradigm for a fully orbed chaplaincy that will serve any correctional facility, regardless of its size, mission, or scope of services. Finally, we provided a schematic for a strategic plan of service delivery that is easily aligned with any institutional mission and that can be effectively monitored for outcomes.

In the process of this exploration, I have challenged certain assumptions within the profession that have often been accepted as axiomatic but which are not well-supported by available data. Additionally, I have identified areas that—if my paradigm is accepted—too many correctional chaplains have either neglected or diminished. I have also pointed to a gradual, but persistent trend of practitioners to validate their institutional roles through administrative functions, a process that has distanced them from their unique pastoral identity.

Correctional chaplaincy is a profession that is clearly at risk. Government at every level—federal, state, and local—faces serious fiscal challenges and too often chaplain positions are easy targets for budgetary cuts. The recognition of this danger has motivated much of the effort within the profession to demonstrate their worth on the basis of their contributions to administrative rather than pastoral functions, and to penological goals at the expense of pastoral pursuits.* This approach fails to address the substantive issues that underlie the erosion of the value once placed on institutional chaplains. Chaplaincy might be better served if, first of all, we did a better job of clearly delineating the full parameters of our role function *as it emerges from our pastoral identity*. Having established that, we must develop a clear path of preparation that prioritizes those skill sets that support those functions. Then, we must create an outcomes-based assessment process that accurately measures those functions and allows for quality management and enhancement of our efforts in specific institutional settings.

PASTORAL IDENTITY

In Chapter Two, we asked a question that must be considered foundational to any apologetic for our profession: *What is it that a chaplain does that no one else in the correctional facility can?* One thing should be clear—unless chaplains provide some distinctive services that differentiate themselves from other social services personnel, they will soon become extinct. After all, some correctional administrators already assert that one doesn't have to have pastoral credentials or be identified as a chaplain to administrate religious programs; they find crucial values in administrative abilities, but view the term "religious" as simply an adjective that needs no interpreter.

> *Chaplains are best qualified to develop and oversee the broad range of religious program options in today's correctional environment because—as pastors—they first of all understand the content of such program material.*

We may argue that chaplains will handle these duties far better than someone with no theological training, but we may not successfully convince a majority of correctional leaders that a trained chaplain is absolutely indispensible in this role. Similarly, we will be hard pressed to claim that only chaplains can offer expert advice in support of RLUIPA–driven questions that correctional administrators confront. In many jurisdictions, that role, too, is being filled by personnel who lack any theological credentials. The religious rights of inmates are legal matters that must be appropriately and fairly addressed by institutional personnel; but while chaplains surely understand the contexts of those things at a level other administrators don't, they are not legal experts and thus their role in such matters is not necessarily an exclusive function of their position.

The paradigm we have presented identifies administration as one of the critical dimensions of chaplaincy and stresses how important this role is in delivering effective ministry programs within correctional facilities. However, our identity must rest fully within the pastoral dimension of the position. We have no reason to be called a *chaplain* if we are no longer keepers of the cloak! Chaplains are best qualified to develop and oversee the broad range of religious program options in today's correctional environment because—as pastors—they first of all understand the content of such program material.

Second, they are experienced practitioners of faith systems who know how religious concepts are best integrated into the life of an individual in a way that fosters positive character development. Finally, their pastoral identity makes them uniquely capable of implementing a strategic plan that incorporates a variety of faith program options that work in a coherent fashion rather than merely filling vacant scheduling slots on the institutional calendar. For these reasons, administrative skills—separated from any pastoral overlay—will always produce less effective and deficient chaplaincy services.

Similarly, the most significant role a professionally functioning chaplain fulfills in ensuring that inmates are able to fully practice the requirements of their faith is not that he or she is completely knowledgeable about every facet of any recognized faith group. First, that is an impossible task; second, there are well-researched and currently maintained documents that any administrator can access to answer such questions. Moreover, correctional administrators also have expert legal resources, many of whom are especially skilled in this arena of law. What chaplains bring to the table is a sensitivity flowing from their ministry-shaped hearts that allows them to accurately decipher spiritual needs of all the inmate population, capably search for resources that can match those needs, and then lovingly facilitate the delivery of those ministry expressions in a "high-touch" manner. Chaplains with a strong pastoral identity realize that ministry delivery is not about legally mandated rights or minimally allowable practices, but it is about spiritual journeys and maximum opportunity to thrive within the context of one's chosen faith. This is never fully satisfied through mere coordination of religious activities.

In our initial exploration of an appropriate chaplaincy paradigm, we observed the slow, yet pervasive movement of chaplaincy away from its core pastoral component and toward role functions defined in terms of their ability to meet institutional needs. In many ways, this parallels a trend toward secularization of most institutions within our Western culture. At the same time, there has been not only a noticeable increase in the number of people who claim the importance of personal faith, but also some substantive documentation that the so-called "faith factor" has power within their lives. Humans are not just physical, psychological, and social beings; they are spiritual beings as well, and that aspect of their makeup is a powerful determinant of individual actions.

In other words, faith works (at some level) for individuals who live by those principles that govern it (see Johnson). Certainly, there has been a significant recent increase in the number of inmates who have been led to practice a multiplicity of faiths, and although there is no shortage of cynicism among some administrators as to the sincerity of their beliefs, chaplains are witnesses of the power of faith to alter the behavior of some of society's most obvious misfits. But neither religious conversion nor the spiritual growth that can transform the offender can be successfully managed by anyone other than a chaplain. Correctional facilities surely need effectively functioning chaplains as members of the programmatic team.

The pastoral role is the only critical dimension of correctional chaplaincy that cannot be filled by someone with no ministry credentials; chaplains alone are positioned within the institution to speak on behalf of a transcendent God and to articulate eternal principles established by Him.

Furthermore, the spiritual dimension is the area of chaplaincy expertise and the locus of their primary contribution within the correctional arena. Their ultimate security rests with this identity; they are irreplaceable unless they willingly forfeit their birthright by settling for lesser responsibilities.

That is not to say the staff position cannot be eliminated by short-sighted officials or the policies they enact, but the pastoral need will always remain, regardless of the staffing pattern employed. Unfortunately, too many chaplains have surrendered their pastoral authority cheaply, and too many correctional officials have been eager to usurp it. Maintaining positions that fail to fulfill the pastoral identity only reinforces and fuels the trend that will eventually eliminate the validity of religious services except as a mandated legal right. Professional chaplains must begin to reverse the current that has carried us far downstream from our legitimate and unique position of influence. That reversal will begin only when we make an intentional commitment to prioritize the pastoral dimension of our ministry.

As early as 1985, in a speech delivered at a regional chaplain's conference, Dr. Charles Riggs, who was at that time the Chaplaincy Services Administrator for the U.S. Bureau of Prisons ended his remarks with these poignant words: "We cannot just sit around idly, moaning or lamenting the state of things while we endure our careers until retirement, only to hear the question, 'Whatever became of prison chaplains like they used to have?' and hear the answer, 'Oh, they went out of business—because they forgot what their business was.' " (Riggs 1985)

May chaplains never forget that they are first and foremost pastors.

PREPARATION

In most professions, there is a clear path of preparation routed through an educational and/or training process that correlates needed knowledge, skills, and abilities with demonstrated job functions. I have pointed out that such is not the case with correctional chaplaincy. Part of the problem lies with the fact that in its early formation, correctional philosophies matched religious views of deviant behavior; thus prisons were constructed and correctional programs designed in ways that were consistent with those assumptions. But as we have seen, those views changed over time as corrections systems restructured under the influence of positivist theories and more nuanced approaches to institutional management.

This has resulted in a constantly shifting role formation for chaplains as they adjusted to changes and attempted to redefine themselves accordingly. As the role of the correctional chaplain has continued to evolve, a disjuncture between preparation and performance has emerged. Once, clinical preparation seemed to offer a solution to this problem, as chaplains interacted with the institutional treatment team to develop collaborative intervention strategies. More recently, the chaplain's knowledge of multiple faith practices and the accompanying legal processes that are required to protect the inmate's rights has become prioritized.

Yet throughout all the reconfiguration, what has not changed is any preplacement educational track that speaks directly to our profession. One of the hazards of trusting the notion that effectiveness is a direct corollary of preparation lies in the assumption that the preparation is structured along lines that relate to specific job tasks. For some reason, we continue to rely on college and seminary training as appropriate and adequate preparation for this career, even though little in their curriculum matches the needs of our institutional duties and the schools show no inclination to serve our profession. Defending the legitimacy of the current degree-based credential as the primary requirement for employment as a chaplain makes little sense.

That is not to say there is no value in such education, or that we should ignore the place of religious training as a core component of chaplaincy preparation. But we must recognize the limitations of this vehicle, accept the fact that most chaplains come to their first assignment without adequate foundations, and be willing to actively support an effort to retool our preparation pathway.

In this text, we have established a paradigm based on core principles of chaplaincy and examined at some length the various functions chaplains are called upon to perform. Along the way, we have referred to many of the skill sets required to successfully accomplish those tasks. What we have not attempted here is any in-depth analysis of the educational components that might lead to competency in these individual areas. But if chaplaincy is to survive as a viable profession beyond the current vagaries within the correctional community, this is a necessity, and it must be given immediate attention.**

As one who has been engaged in the training of correctional ministers more than twenty-five years, I am struck by the lack of any sustained cooperative involvement to address this matter. Many chaplains talk about the lack of concern demonstrated by their respective denominations and the educational institutions those entities support and sustain, yet I can point to no concerted efforts by any coalition of chaplains to advocate for this needed accommodation or to develop a proposal to remedy the situation. Why have we been content to struggle through our professional lives without working to improve our credentialing process and thus improving the potential of those who follow us into the correctional arena? We need to engage a task force, recruited from a broad cross-section of working chaplains and at least one educational institution, to attack this problem and create a viable educational process that equips one to effectively perform the tasks we have identified.

> *Absent any overarching certification requirement or broadly accepted performance standards, chaplains have little reason to participate in an agenda for professional development and little to choose from by way of targeted skill enhancement.*

Once the front end has been established, we then need to address the delivery of continuing education opportunities. Here, too, there is serious deficiency. Part of the problem, of course, is that there are dwindling resources available for any training venture. Another part is attitudinal in nature; having "arrived" by virtue of an appointment as chaplain, there is little motivation to add to one's toolbox of skills if there is no professional motivation or institutional requirement to do so. Absent any overarching certification requirement or broadly accepted performance standards, chaplains have little reason to participate in an agenda for professional development and little to choose from by way of targeted skill enhancement.

Regional chaplaincy meetings offer some worthwhile engagements, but those are sometimes sporadically delivered and reflect no cohesive agreed-upon professional agendas. Until these items are addressed, chaplaincy will continue to stand apart from other social service professionals that have well-refined continuing educational tracks and specific annual CEU requirements that serve to sharpen needed skill sets and dispense new information relevant to the job.

It is easy to fall back on the claim that we lack funds to create continuing educational opportunities, but given the technology available today, that excuse is quickly invalidated. We can capably develop and inexpensively deliver useful educational products to a wide-ranging group of professionals. What is lacking is:

- The determination to create such a vehicle
- Our willingness to meaningfully collaborate with each other to develop a product that reflects functional best practices
- The time and energy it will take to develop the training modules
- A partnership with an educational provider that can provide both technical assistance and pedagogical expertise

The point of all this is to underscore the fact that our understanding of the diverse set of gifts and skills essential for the making and cultivation of an effective correctional chaplain doesn't rest with any single competency or knowledge base. We have described the chaplain as an individual who, ideally, is grounded with a strong religious education, but who also has training in psychology and criminology; who understands management principles; possesses facilitation skills; is interpersonally effective; and who is a competent counselor.

We should not rely on religious education or credentials alone as the ultimate determiner of employment, nor should we adopt the stance that whatever front-end requirements we pose automatically establish one as a trained professional. To repeat myself—professionalism is a functional behavior that is measured by performance rather than preparation. This means, then, that after initial employment, a strong program of continuing education is vital if we hope to achieve any quality control of chaplaincy service delivery.

PERFORMANCE

In discussing chaplaincy performance, we must acknowledge two contradictory impulses at work within the correctional arena. First, a commitment to evidence-based practices currently drives programmatic decision making in most criminal justice environments, both in-house and with contracted services. Yet chaplains have been slow to embrace assessments of their effectiveness based along these lines, and use some sort of quantitative measures of their activities rather than to qualitative assessments when validating their work. They produce statistics to show how many services they have facilitated, the number of inmates who participate in religious activities, how many volunteers their departments have managed, the number of inmate requests handled, and other similar quantifications to demonstrate their value. Some chaplaincy departments have even calculated the dollar amount of services rendered by the volunteers they supervise as a way of calculating the net institutional worth of chaplaincy programs.

But all such quantifications only measure *output* (energy expended) rather than *outcome* (achievement). Working hard and being committed to a redemptive purpose are not the same thing as effectiveness in tasks that fulfill specific mission goals, a standard by which most other correctional professionals are evaluated. Though there have been some discussions about the value of chaplains and their programs, those discussions have remained primarily theoretical and chaplains themselves have seldom been subjected to any performance-based rubric.

There are several reasons for this. In the first place, it is always easier to count items than to measure human activity; the process is simple, and the results are precise and easily verified. Second, without any broad agreement either within professional ranks or among different correctional agencies about the precise roles of chaplains or what their efforts are expected to deliver, we can't begin to measure effectiveness, anyway. In both these instances, the failure of chaplains to create a more substantial and sustainable platform of performance for themselves has served to undermine their institutional footing and make it that much easier for correctional departments to substitute inappropriate personnel without faith credentials or applied experience for bona fide chaplains.

There is a third factor, however, that may have caused chaplains to hesitate placing their activities under the traditional social science performance model: The fact that a good deal of what takes place in the spiritual realm simply cannot be measured. As Jesus pointed out to Nicodemus, "The wind blows wherever it pleases. You hear its sound, but you cannot tell where it comes from or where it is going. So it is with everyone born of the Spirit" (*John 3:8–9*). We should note that although Jesus indicates here that the source of the Spirit is mysterious and its actions not humanly controllable, He does describe some of its behaviors as observable, and we can therefore extrapolate that they are in some sense measurable.

> *The field of correctional chaplaincy desperately needs to develop an assessment process that will fairly and accurately measure the programs chaplains administrate or personally deliver in terms of identifiable outcome goals for the recipients.*

Still, few chaplaincy departments have adopted an outcomes-based assessment of the programs they supervise (the Bureau of Prisons is one exception). Most of what is being done in this regard takes place in the area of individual faith and character units within prisons to which a greater measure of rigor is maintained and a higher degree of outcomes expected (Indiana and Florida's programs are examples of this). Yet the field of correctional chaplaincy desperately needs to develop an assessment process that will fairly and accurately measure the programs chaplains administrate or personally deliver in terms of identifiable outcome goals for the recipients.

This will not be an easy task and may only be achievable within individual correctional systems or isolated jail jurisdictions, but information about the models that are developed, assessment tools created, and criteria employed can then be widely disseminated to other agencies for adoption or refinement as appropriate. The resulting dialogue should allow us to build on shared successes or failures and significantly enhance our profession.

Although program outcomes will measure one segment of a chaplain's performance, they don't tell the entire story. Previously, we have argued that preparation and whatever credentials one brings to the job of chaplaincy are not necessarily related to successful role function, and we have presented the critical dimensions of chaplaincy within which all the day-to-day functions of the position reside. We have also outlined an approach to developing an individualized ministry plan for the specific institution in which any chaplain is placed. Once that plan is completed and the specific facility goals established, a clear set of outcomes are now in place that allows for the measurement of the chaplain's competencies on the basis of those deliverables.

These metrics permit us to evaluate the effectiveness of role demands independent of program dynamics, and to separate performance of the chaplain from the components of those programs. Good programs may be poorly administered, but they may also simply be poorly designed for the intended purposes; using this tool can help us understand which is which. It will also help us determine what areas within the total chaplaincy job description the chaplain excels in; which areas he or she may be deficient; and thus pinpoint the places where skill enhancement is most needed. Finally, it subjects chaplains to a system of accountability that is not based on past preparation, previously acquired credentials, or any assumed professionalism based solely on job appointment. Excellence in performance will be the only standard by which chaplains can be measured—as it should be.

One caveat is essential to note: Much of the work of faith will remain unquantifiable. We simply cannot put God in a box, and though we can measure some of the results of spiritually driven behavioral change, we cannot adequately measure much that lies in the spiritual domain. However, if we have faithfully approached the ministry of chaplaincy from a pastoral perspective and have designed a strategic plan to address the breadth of our service delivery, we can establish metrics that tell us whether or not we have accomplished the objectives we established. We can then leave accountability of the spiritual accomplishments to the God we serve.

PARISH: THE MISSING LINK

In Chapter One, we reviewed the early history of the Church's involvement with correctional institutions, pointing out the religious principles that influenced penological practices within our country's first prison systems, as well as the role of our first prison and jail chaplains. But with the specialization of prison staffing and the development of national organizations devoted to the professionalization of the corrections industry, the Church rapidly abandoned any primary engagement in this arena.

Today, the Roman Catholic Church and most mainline Protestant denominations have retained offices that address issues of social or criminal justice and other specialized ministries, and usually they have some sort of ancillary administrative arm to facilitate those of their pastors who have chosen chaplaincy for their field of ministry endeavor. There are some denominations that, like their Roman Catholic counterpart, embrace the parish concept and—at least officially—direct their pastors to serve any prison population that lies within the geographic confines of that parish. Practically, however, little is delivered by way of any direct pastoral services to those institutions without the persistent urging of a local chaplain or one of their parishioners. Even that voice is rarely able to compete with those other, more palatable, ministry demands.

> *In essence, all prison and jail ministry—whether conducted by a professional chaplain or by a volunteer who addresses an isolated program need—is treated as mission work and relegated to occasional publicity and sporadic support of any kind. With few exceptions, churches of all varieties are wired only to serve free-world communities.*

Seldom do ecclesiastically initiated chaplaincy assignments take place. The positions are acceptable when acquired by the pastor, and the Church hierarchies then oversee the continuation of the placement by way of annual review and endorsements, but in only a few isolated cases does the Church actually employ the pastor for the work of correctional chaplaincy or direct him or her to undertake such an assignment. In essence, all prison and jail ministry—whether conducted by a professional chaplain or by a volunteer who addresses an isolated program need—is treated as mission work and relegated to occasional publicity and sporadic support of any kind. With few exceptions, churches of all varieties are wired only to serve free-world communities. In one regard, this is the same disconnect that exists with any number of social ministry needs that were once addressed by the Church, but which have long since been grafted into our network of tax-funded and publically operated social services. It is easy for the church to neglect those things that most of its parishioners accept as being competently addressed through their tax dollars.

In this text, I have made a strong case that the correctional chaplain's pastoral role has been considerably minimized in recent years, and that unless we are able to find our way back to a place where we can fully exercise that role, the title of Chaplain will cease to have any inherently religious meaning, and our unique contribution to correctional facilities will be lost. But that statement is true only if the basis of our position and our call to ministry rests with the Church instead of the State. Chaplains cannot be ambassadors for God unless they are sent from His Church and fill a valid ministry role ordained by that Body; they cannot obtain pastoral authority from a governmental entity, and that authority can't be delegated by the Church to the government. So where does that leave us?

Chaplains and Church leadership must quickly open a dialogue to identify concrete steps toward a legitimate merger of ministry efforts. From the macro perspective of the Church, chaplains serve a certain subset of individuals, caught up in a web of destructive behaviors that damage themselves, others around them, and—ultimately—societal structures. Thus, both perpetrators and victims of crimes, along with those institutions within our communities that are impacted by crime, comprise a significant portion of those whom the Church is called to offer redemption and healing. The correctional chaplain occupies a pivotal point along the axis of crime, and as such, the Church should consider him or her a key player in their plan to engage a hurting and needy world.

At the same time, chaplains need to acknowledge anew the sacred source of our pastoral call and adjust our understandings accordingly. Our interaction with the leadership of our faith groups will have to reach beyond periodic token reports and annual reappointments, and we must hold ourselves accountable for ministry outcomes that have potential to bear real fruit when we pass along those men and women God has given through our correctional position to our coworkers in churches beyond the walls.

Studies consistently verify the role of community as a strong predictor of lasting behavioral change. In prisons, a vibrant community of inmate believers has significant power to help each other adjust to their environment, and has also been positively correlated with fewer disciplinary infractions. Upon release, when ex-offenders become meaningfully assimilated into supportive faith groups outside the prison, their rate of re-cidivism is also reduced. This points to a primary nexus for chaplains and the Church from which re-entry services can begin. Some state corrections departments—Oregon, Colorado, and most recently, Texas—have followed the lead of our Canadian neighbors and recruited community-based chaplains to assist with reentry processes. To this point, though, few churches are eagerly embracing this opportunity, which provides another reason for chaplains to understand and fulfill the community dimension of chaplaincy we elaborated on in Chapter Eight. There does appear to be a window of opportunity that has opened for chaplains to speak propheti-cally to the Church, calling it back to a ministry near to God's heart and which rests far more closely to the center of the Church's mission than it may want to acknowledge.

*An informative website is: http://www.preciousheart.net/Save_Chaplaincy.htm main-tained by Texas chaplain Michael Maness. Here the reader can follow a recent legislative battle over the budgeting of chaplaincy positions in that state and track the arguments made in support of chaplaincy services. Chaplain Maness maintains the most complete data base of chaplaincy activities I have encountered.

** To view a curriculum I developed specifically for chaplaincy education, go to: http://www.bgcprisonministries.com/assets/files/Correctional%20Chaplaincy%20Credential%20Program%20Requirements.pdf. This one component of a more comprehensive program offered by the *School of Correctional Ministries* through the Institute for Prison Ministries at Wheaton College (http://www.bgcprisonministries.com/).

REFERENCES

Johnson, Byron R. (2011). *More God, Less Crime*. West Conshohocken, PA: Templeton Press.

STATE	HIGH SCHOOL	B. A. /B.S.	SEMINARY OR MASTERS	PASTORAL EXP	PRISC EXP
ALABAMA					
Chaplain		X		Some	
ALASKA					
Chaplaincy Program Coordinator		X			Some
Institutional Chaplain					Some
Vol. Facility Chaplain					Some
ARIZONA					
Corr. Chaplain I				2 Years	
Corr. Chaplain II					2Yrs. as Corr. Chaplai
Or for Chap. II			X		
ARKANSAS					
Chaplain		X			1 Yea
Sr. Chaplain		X			2 Year
CALIFORNIA					
Protestant Chaplain		X		2 Years	
Catholic Chaplain					
Jewish Chaplain				2 Years	
Muslim Chaplain					
Native American Spiritual Leader				2 Years as recognized Native Am. Spiritual Leader	
COLORADO					
*					
CONNECTICUT					
Chaplain			X	1 Year	
Assoc. Chaplain			X	3 Years	

CHAPLAINCY QUALIFICATIONS (2002)

ORDINATION	ENDORSEMENT	CPE/ SUPVERVISED MINISTRY	SPECIAL
X	X		Plus participation in grad. theol. training program
X			Plus completion of theological studies sufficient for ordination; Management & administrative exp. & training; Correctional chaplaincy adm. desirable
X			Partially state funded - Contracted
X			
X	X		
		4 Units	
X	X	4 Units	CPE units or 3 yrs. of supervised pastoral training
	X		Other job related ed. and/or exp. may be substituted for all or part of these basic requirements
	X		Other job related ed. and/or exp. may be substituted for all or part of these basic requirements
X		4 quarters or 2 yrs supv. training in ministry or social science field	1) Ed. must contain min of 12 sem units in counseling, psychology or related field. 2) Each year of graduate ed may substitute for 3 months CPE or 6 months of field training (max 2 quarters CPE or 6 months training
X	By Diocese		Completion of theol. Studies for ordination as a Priest
X		4 quarters or 2 yrs supv training in ministry or social science field or 1 yr with National Jewish Welfare Board	Completion of theol. Studies for ordination as a Rabbi; and equivalent to BA with 12 sem. Units in counseling, psychology or related field
	Certification by local resident Imam	Equivalent of 1 yr full-time supv. field training	Education: Completion of 2 yrs of Islamic Religious Studies
	Certification by his/her tribe		
			NO CHAPLAINS EMPLOYED; ALL VOLUNTEER SYSTEM, WITH FULL-TIME CHAPLAINS PROVIDED BY PRIVATE VENDORS
X	X	2 Units (may complete within 3 years of employment)	Completion of formal religious training recognized by denomination which include completion of 4 yr. degree may be substituted for general experience; Completion of all formal religious training required by denomination may substitute for Master's level training
X	X	4 Units (2 advanced)	Completion of formal religious training recognized by denomination which include completion of 4 yr. degree may be substituted for general experience; Completion of all formal religious training required by denomination may substitute for Master's level training

STATE	HIGH SCHOOL	B. A. /B.S.	SEMINARY OR MASTERS	PASTORAL EXP	PRIS EX
FED BUREAU OF PRISONS					
Chaplain			X	2 Years	
FLORIDA					
Chaplain		X		1 Year	
Sr. Chaplain		X		2 Years	
GEORGIA					
Chaplain 1		X		Some	
Or Chaplain I				3 Years Post Ordination	
INDIANA					
Chaplain III			X	3 Years	
IOWA					
Chaplain					
KANSAS					
Clinical Chaplain					
KENTUCKY					
Chaplain			X		
LOUISIANA					
Chaplain I		X	X		
MARYLAND					
Chaplain					
MASSACHUSETTS					
Chaplain					
MICHIGAN					
Chaplain		X			

RDIN-TION	ENDORSE-MENT	CPE/ SUPVERVISED MINISTRY	SPECIAL
	X		1) Educational equivalency for graduate degree: 90 semester hours distributed within prescribed academic areas 2) CPE may satisfy up to 1 yr of req. of pastoral experience
X	X		
X	X		
			All positions are part-time; contracted
X	Or X	Some	3 additional position levels exist, with higher hourly pay for each position Minimal requirements increase for higher levels
X	X	1 Unit or completion of supv counseling practicum	
		4 quarters	OR exp. equal to 1 yr of full-time chaplain/minister/youth leader will substitute for CPE OR any equivalent combination of CPE and full-time work
	X	Some or equivalent specialized training	
X	X	1 Unit	Exp. as ordained minister will substitute for the required education on a year-for-year basis.
	X	4 Units (or specialized experience)	1) Must be certified by LA Chaplains Association 2) Chaplain II, III, IV, which signify increased responsibilities, have same minimal requirements except for years of experience as Chaplain
			Chaplains are full-time state employees, full-time contractual employees, and part-time contractual employees. All have the same minimal requirements: "The training and education required by their denomination in order to perform sacraments."
	X	1 Unit or equivalent	Selection of Chaplains is on the basis of " the ability to meet the spiritual needs of prisoners." While indicators of that ability may be education or experience, no minimal requirements are mandated for positions
	X		4 levels of chaplains exist, each higher level requires a minimum of 1 year in order to be reallocated to next level. Requirements remain the same.

STATE	HIGH SCHOOL	B. A. /B.S.	SEMINARY OR MASTERS	PASTORAL EXP	PRIS EX
MINNESOTA					
Religious Serv. Coor.		X			
MISSISSIPPI					
Chaplain I			X		
OR		X			1 Ye
Chaplain II			X		1 Ye
OR		X			2 Yea
Chaplain III			X		2 Yea
OR		X			3 Yea
MISSOURI					
Chaplain		X		2 Years	
MONTANA					
Chaplain			X*	5 Years*	
NEBRASKA					
Religious Coor. I	*				
Religious Coor. II	*				
NEW JERSEY					
Assoc. Chaplain					
Chaplain		X			
NEW YORK					
Chaplain					
NORTH CAROLINA					
Clinical Chaplain I,II,III			X	*	
Chaplain Associate		X		2 Years	
Chaplain Trainee I		X			
Chaplain Trainee II			X		
Community Funded/Vol. Chaplain					
OHIO					
Chaplain		X		1 Year	
OKLAHOMA					
Chaplain Level I			X	1 Year	
OR		X		3 Years	
OR					
Chaplain Level II					
OREGON					
Chaplain			X	3 Years	

APLAINCY QUALIFICATIONS (2002)

RDIN-TION	ENDORSE-MENT	CPE/ SUPERVISED MINISTRY	SPECIAL
			Specialized training in theology/related field may substitute for degree
X	X		
X	X		
X	X		
X	X		
X	X		
X	X		
	X		1yr. of acceptable pastoral/work ex. May be substituted for each year min education req. not met
X*			*No minimal requirements are specifically mandated; but duties and responsibilities of the position are "typically acquired" through fulfillment of these requirements
			*Post high school coursework and/or experience in behavioral sciences
			*Post high school coursework and/or experience in behavioral sciences
X	X	1 yr. or equivalent	
X	X	1 yr. or equivalent	Supervisory chaplain requires Master's Degree & 2 yrs. Supervisory experience
	X		
X	X	4 Units or equivalency	Full-time state paid Clinical Chaplain I may also be contracted *Clinical Chaplain II req. 2 years of institutional exp. *Clinical Chaplain III req. 3 years of institutional exp.
X	X		Contract Only
			Contract only, enrolled in an accredited sem./school of theology
X	X	Enrolled	Contract only
			May be part-time or full-time.
X		1 Unit	
	X		
			Equivalent combination of ed. & exp. –Substitute 1 month of CPE for each month of required experience
			Same as Level I plus 2 yrs. of qualifying exp. Or equivalent combination of ed. & exp. Substituting 1 month of CPE for each month of required experience
X	X		Professional/formal, full-time, resident religious training of a similar nature will be considered as equivalent to seminary or theological school.

STATE	HIGH SCHOOL	B. A. /B.S.	SEMINARY OR MASTERS	PASTORAL EXP	PRIS EX
PENNSYLVANIA					
Facility Chaplain Program Director			X		1 Yea
Chaplain					
SOUTH CAROLINA					
Clinical Chaplain			X	1 Year	
SOUTH DAKOTA					
*					
TENNESSEE					
Chaplain			X		
TEXAS					
Chaplain			X	2 Years	
OR		X		4 Years	
OR	X			8 Years	
UTAH					
Chaplain		X*			
VERMONT					
*					
VIRGINIA					
Staff Chaplain*			X	3 Years	
WASHINGTON					
Chaplain Specialist		X		2 Years	
Chaplain, Chaplain Manager, Chaplain Supervisor			X		
WEST VIRGINIA					
Chaplain		X			
WISCONSIN					
Chaplain	X				
WYOMING					
Chaplain		X		3 Years	
WY CHURCH COALITION*			X		

NOTE: Categories with no designation indicate no stated requirement.

CHAPLAINCY QUALIFICATIONS (2002)

ORDIN-ATION	ENDORSE-MENT	CPE/ SUPVERVISED MINISTRY	SPECIAL
			Part-time contractual positions are also utilized for specific faith groups
	X		OR 1 yr. of formal chaplaincy training will substitute for experience
	X		Any equivalent combination of exp. & training which provides the required knowledge/skills
X	X	4 Units	
			*NO CHAPLAINS EMPLOYED; ALL VOLUNTEER SYSTEM
X	X		Substitute: qualifying full-time professional pastoral experience may be substituted for the required education on a year-for-year basis to the max. of 2 yrs.
	X		
	X		
	X		30 semester hours may be substituted for 1 year exp.
			*Presumed but not specifically required. All chaplains are part-time; contracted
			* NO CHAPLAINS EMPLOYED; ALL VOLUNTEER SYSTEM
X	X	1 Unit	* All chaplains provided by Chaplain Service of the Churches of Virginia, Inc.
		1 Year supervised faith group training	This position hired to provide spiritual leadership of specific faith groups, e.g. Native Americans
X (or cognized religious leader)	X		
X	Or X		May substitute graduation from high school and 5 yrs experience in pastoral counseling or religious ministry for Bachelor's Degree
	X	1 Year (supervised institutional training	
X	X	4 Units	*Places chaplains in Wyoming State Prisons